PITMAN EDUCATION SERIES
Rychard Fink, General Editor

PITMAN EDUCATION SERIES

Richard Fink, General Editor

ELEMENTARY SCIENCE: A BOOK OF READINGS
Edited by Robert E. Carroll

GROUPING IN THE ELEMENTARY SCHOOL
Edited by Anne Morgenstern

THE MASTER TEACHER AND THE ART OF TEACHING
John E. Colman, C.M.

NEW PERSPECTIVES IN READING INSTRUCTION
Edited by Albert J. Mazurkiewicz

SKETCH STORIES FOR CHALK TALK
Daniel Sugarman and Zelma Healdman

TEACHING HISTORY AND THE SOCIAL STUDIES
IN SECONDARY SCHOOLS
Osyth Lewis and David Edris

Teacher-Pupil Planning
FOR BETTER CLASSROOM LEARNING

Teacher-Pupil Planning
FOR BETTER CLASSROOM LEARNING

YVONNE WASKIN

Michigan State University

LOUISE PARRISH

Muskegon County Community College

Pitman Publishing Corporation
New York · Toronto · London

© 1967 by Pitman Publishing Corporation
Library of Congress Catalog Card Number: 66-25739
Design by Anita Karl
Manufactured in the United States of America
1.987654321

Dedicated to our colleagues in Michigan

PREFACE

Teacher-pupil planning is one practical answer to the modern need for meaningful classroom experience. But, you ask, how is it done? How can I, who have had experience and example only in the more traditional methods, begin such apparently drastic methods in my classes? To these questions and to others we hope to give some answers in this book, answers we found while working with pupils in our own classrooms.

Although teacher-pupil planning can be used in any class, we believe it is most successful in a class that offers more than one period a day for teachers and pupils to be together. Most of the descriptions in this book are taken from two- and three-hour classes. The classroom experiences described are taken from seventh, ninth, and tenth grade levels and are of two different types. One consists of a block of time with no subject matter barriers; it replaces the English class and the social studies courses. Another type of class has a stipulation of subject matter. It is a ninth grade class that meets for three hours for English, civics, social living, and homeroom. The correlation possibilities of these subjects are excellent, and the content offers a wide range of working areas.

The techniques described in this book can be used at any grade level from kindergarten through the high school. They have been tried and found to be successful and profitable even in the classrooms of many universities. They have also been used very effectively with adult groups working on projects unrelated to education. Indeed, the basic tenet of teacher-pupil planning, of helping people to plan, work, and evaluate cooperatively, can be utilized in almost any situation.

In past years we have been active in Michigan curriculum circles, having participated in the annual Core Conference, sponsored by the Michigan Department of Education and the National Core

Conference, sponsored by a group of educators interested in core programs. We have acted as consultants at many curriculum conferences, in university classrooms, and for school systems initiating core programs. We have consulted informally with innumerable teachers who felt concerned about the kinds of educational problems dealt with here. Our teaching experience has included teaching in junior high school, junior college, and university classes.

The material in this book is based upon questions we have discussed with teachers in the field. We hope that many teachers will recognize in these descriptions methods approximating those which they, like all good teachers, have used, for they will then have faith in our other suggestions. We hope, too, that we may give courage to teachers to try out new ideas and to bring pupils into the planning. Our purpose in writing this book is to share our experiences with others. We have found that teacher-pupil planning can be exciting, challenging, and rewarding, and we feel that our use of these methods contributes in some small way to the building of responsible, informed citizens and the preservation of democratic ideals.

We are indebted to many people for the impetus that has enabled us to write this book. Dr. Earl C. Kelly of Wayne State University especially deserves our thanks for his help with the final manuscript, as well as Dr. Roland Faunce, also of Wayne, who gave us the initial encouragement to do the writing. We appreciate the inspiration from the many classroom teachers whose stimulating questions and ideas have reinforced and clarified our thinking.

CONTENTS

Teacher-Pupil Planning
FOR BETTER CLASSROOM LEARNING

CHAPTER 1

Introduction

Education has followed a pattern of teacher-planned, teacher-dominated classrooms, the type in which most of us had our school experience from kindergarten through college. The average classroom of the past often had for the learner little relationship to the realities of the outside world.

In his book, *Education for What Is Real,* Dr. Earl C. Kelley lists some assumptions that seem to be deeply imbedded in the educational thinking of the past. One is "that education is supplementary to and preparatory to life, not life itself." To illustrate this point Dr. Kelley says:

> Since education is supplementary and preparatory, we build school buildings designed to shut out life so that the child can give complete attention to our abstractions or tools for conveying these abstractions, to books, to blackboards, and chalk. The windows of the classroom are often purposely built high so that the child cannot look out of them and be distracted.[1]

Modern school design, fortunately, is moving away from the earlier custom of shutting out the outside world. Teaching practice should become as functional for life as the latest in building design.

Classroom methods of the past that gave little heed to life experiences have without doubt fulfilled many needs, but we must ask ourselves how meaningful they have been to the great number of people who are products of our schools. We often hear regret expressed by former students that they did not "get more out of school," the implication being that this was the fault of the individual. We wonder, however, whether the school may not have been at fault even more, since school experiences were not more meaningful to the potential learner.

We believe that school experiences must relate to real life. The demands of a fast-moving modern society are not waiting for educa-

[1] Earl C. Kelley, *Education for What Is Real* (New York, Harper & Brothers, 1947), pp. 18-19.

tion to relate school experiences to reality. We of the educational world must find better ways of working with children, ways that help them to meet the challenge of today's world. It is imperative that we find and use these methods now, before it is too late. Already the threat of destruction hangs over us. We believe in democracy and the democratic way of life. We believe in the worth and dignity of the individual and his inherent right to "life, liberty, and the pursuit of happiness." We realize that the success or failure of democratic government depends on the individual and his willingness and capability to accept the responsibility of participation in his government. All this we believe, and yet these beliefs which we accept in terms of government, beliefs for which Americans have worked and sacrificed, have rarely been put into educational practice.

In the nation's classrooms exists the greatest opportunity to teach children to live democratically. The possibilities for creating situations where students can practice democratic living have barely been tapped.

The mastery of certain skills is imperative if one is to live happily, successfully, and productively in a democratic society. These skills can be learned only through experience. Given the opportunity, children can learn the skills of:

1. Participation—They must be capable of participating intelligently in activities that concern them.
2. Accepting responsibility—They must be able to accept responsibility for their own actions and for obligations placed upon them by their society.
3. Cooperation—They must be capable of helping others and of letting others have a say in what transpires.
4. Understanding—They must be aware of the problems that face others and look upon them with a spirit of understanding and helpfulness.
5. Problem solving—They must be capable of recognizing problems and of planning a course of action leading to solutions.
6. Acquiring knowledge—They must learn how to obtain information that will help them in their everyday living. They must have a factual background of information to support their beliefs and opinions, to increase their understanding, and to enable them to solve problems.

The mastery of these skills can lead to the development of outstanding citizens. How can we best ascertain that these skills are mastered by our students? Is lecturing about good citizenship and its place in a democratic society effective enough? We know that it is not. We have only to look about us and observe the apathy among our citizens toward assuming responsibility in government and toward their fellow men to see that some other methods must be utilized if democracy is to continue to exist.

George B. de Huszar, in his book *Practical Applications of Democracy*, says:

> Citizenship cannot be taught. It is a skill which must be acquired by constant practice; it is the attainment of certain attitudes and habits of action which make democratic living together possible . . . and how can we expect democratic results from authoritarian processes in education? We often try what cannot be done: to attain one kind of end by another kind of means. . . . We need an educational system which is democratic in structure which will build human beings capable of living together, rather than dominating each other.[2]

We believe that the skills necessary for democratic living can be learned in a classroom. No one person needs to be dominant, but rather each individual contributes what he can to the success of each undertaking. If students are to learn to live democratically they must have a voice in how they shall spend their time. They must be included in determining their needs and interests. In other words, they must be included in the planning of the work they shall undertake.

"Teacher-pupil planning" is a phrase now frequently used in educational circles. It means planning educational activities with pupils so that the needs and desires they have and recognize are taken into consideration. It means that the teacher is constantly alert to see that the needs she knows exist for her students are also met. It means that teachers and pupils *plan, work, evaluate* together —and that in this process the skills necessary for democratic living are gradually developed.

[2] George B. de Huszar, *Practical Applications of Democracy* (New York, Harper & Brothers, 1947), pp. 52, 56.

CHAPTER 2

A Preview

Bill Adams wanted to observe a classroom where teacher-pupil planning was being used. He had heard about this procedure and read about it, and he was curious to see a real demonstration. His principal suggested that he take a day off to visit a teacher in another school who was reportedly using teacher-pupil planning techniques with a large degree of success. Bill made arrangements through the principal to visit a seventh grade class entitled simply "general education."

Like many other teachers, Bill pictured teacher-pupil planning as an unstructured process in which the students did as they pleased without much interference from the teacher. It was with a good deal of skepticism that he approached the designated room just before class was to begin. Pupils were milling about in the hall and there was a good deal of the general scurry which inevitably accompanies the last few minutes of the noon hour. Bill stepped into the room, glancing about him. He sensed immediately that here was something different from what he had anticipated.

Boys and girls were visiting casually together making various preparations for class to begin. They seemed to be well acquainted and interested in one another. Bill noticed they were not quiet, but he heard none of the raucous noise that often is heard before a class is called to order. Mr. Adams' mental picture of the schoolroom he had expected to find underwent considerable change in those few quick glances.

He spotted the teacher talking with two boys. When he approached her she greeted him cordially, introducing herself as Miss Johnson. He was introduced at once to the two boys beside her and she asked them to take care of him during the afternoon. Mr. Adams was surprised at this development since he had planned to spend his time with the teacher, but he obligingly followed his new acquaintances as they ushered him to a table and found him a chair among several other students.

While they were settling themselves at the table, Mr. Adams

heard the usual bell in the hall, calling school into session for the afternoon. The students in general education seated themselves around the tables. A boy said, "Will the class please come to order?"

The classroom quieted down and the same boy went on, "Will the secretary please take the roll?"

A girl sitting beside the chairman began calling the various names, writing on the absence slip the name of one girl who did not answer.

"This is the day for our regular business meeting, so is there any business to bring up?"

Several hands were raised quickly. When the chairman called on a girl named Lois she reported that the committee working on the candy sale for next Thursday had made all the necessary plans. Any member of the group who could contribute fudge made at home was asked to sign his name on the list tacked to a bulletin board near the door.

Frank, who was called on next, said that he noticed Jane had been absent for four days; he wondered whether the class shouldn't find out what was the matter and perhaps send her a gift if she were ill.

A discussion developed and finally the chairman asked whether some pupils would volunteer to take care of the matter. He chose three from among the volunteers and then asked for further business. The treasurer's report was heard, the student council representative reported on the last council meeting, the daily announcements from the office were read, and the chairman then stated, "If there is no further business, the meeting is adjourned and we'll have the chairman of the planning committee, Jack Edwards, take over."

While the meeting was being held Bill Adams took the opportunity to look around the room more carefully. The bulletin boards, he noticed, were not just for pictures put up by the teacher. Each section was devoted to a meaningful display of illustrations and information dealing with some specific topic. They were attractively arranged and labeled; one or two were as yet unfinished. All showed that the pupils had done the work, some more skillfully than others. Two sections were devoted to general information and announcements for the two general education classes that used the room. One bulletin board section on the side wall was covered with newspaper clippings of current news events. Another small section near the door displayed cartoons of various kinds. Mr. Adams made a mental note to examine all of these more carefully.

All the available bookcase space in the room was crowded with a variety of reading material consisting of pamphlets, magazines, newspapers, books on manners for teen-agers, and books of general interest. An orange-crate bookcase against the front blackboard was labeled "Lending Library" and held juvenile fiction books that obviously belonged to the students. In one large glass-front bookcase were several groups of textbooks, dictionaries, and encyclopedias, plus many other volumes of reference material and general information.

Mr. Adams' attention was returned to the front of the room when the chairman of the planning committee began to speak. Jack stepped over to the blackboard where a weekly schedule, arranged by days and hours, had been cleverly designed in colored chalk.

"First on the agenda today," he said, "is current events. Martha is the discussion leader. Then we're going to work on research for our projects. Some kids have interviews arranged and some have to go to the library. After that, we're going to have a discussion of the story we read in the literature books yesterday. Then the last ten minutes two of the girls are going to teach us a new song they learned in Girl Scouts. That's all for today, but don't forget that your progress reports are due today. Any questions? O.K., Martha, we'll start with current events."

With that, Jack took his seat and Martha pulled a chair up to the front of the room. Mr. Adams marveled at the ease with which the pupils spoke, their composure, and their genuine interest in the activities of the group. He looked around to see what Miss Johnson had been doing all this time and saw that she was sitting at a table with some of the pupils, relaxed but alert to every occurrence. He remembered then that she had spoken only once or twice, once to straighten out a point in the student council report, and once to suggest that the chairman choose volunteers for a committee instead of having some students elected who didn't care to serve. She remained unobtrusively in the background, and yet, as Mr. Adams realized, her presence was a vital factor in the smooth operation of the class.

Following the current events discussion, Martha directed the students to move into their working groups, and as the general session broke up Mr. Adams moved toward Miss Johnson. She suggested that he might like to sit in on one of the working groups or look at some of the materials in the room. He stood aside as she signed library permits for several pupils and hall permits for several others who were on their way to the local police department to interview some of the law enforcement officers in connection with their projects.

The transition period from the general session to working groups was made without undue confusion. Everyone was moving around at once—some were in and out of the room, others were busy getting out materials for their projects. One girl set up a typewriter on a back table and began pecking away industriously. Two other girls busied themselves with library cards from a file in the front of the room. Students helped themselves to materials from the filing cabinet and bookshelves. A great deal of chatter and moving of furniture went on, and yet the noise all this activity caused created a purposeful hum in the room. Two boys began arguing about the way a display should be arranged, and though Miss Johnson noticed them she said nothing. Within a few moments the point was settled to their mutual satisfaction.

Bill Adams walked around the room when he saw that Miss Johnson had seated herself with one of the groups. He watched her and her students while she talked with them. Her genuine interest in them was reflected in their reactions to her. She was pleasant and composed and her pupils responded in kind. She made several suggestions as to how they might improve what they were doing. At no time did she attempt to impose her demands upon the pupils. The atmosphere was one of helpful cooperation and meaningful activity.

At one point the bell rang again and several students left the room to join the throngs in the hall. Others remained at their work momentarily and then sauntered out. Some didn't leave the room at all. After five minutes the students returned to their work without prompting and the break allowed them was over. Mr. Adams was amazed that the usual stampede to get out and then to get back in again had not taken place. He was further amazed when another teacher called Miss Johnson out of the room for about ten minutes and apparently no one noticed her absence.

As the time for the discussion of the story approached, Jack Edwards, the chairman of the planning committee, came up to Miss Johnson. Mr. Adams heard him say that the pupils who went to the police station had not returned and so there could be no discussion because some of them were on the panel. What were they to do with that time? Where were the interviewers? Miss Johnson calmly suggested that they were undoubtedly delayed for some good reason. She suggested that the remaining time might well be spent continuing project work and completing the progress reports. Jack agreed with this and promptly began his rounds of the room to tell the others. He then called the planning committee out into the hall and motioned to Miss Johnson to join them. She went out and returned in a few minutes to explain to her visitor that plans for tomorrow had to be revised somewhat to accommodate today's changes.

Before long it was time to clean up the room in preparation for the song the pupils were to learn. Miss Johnson asked some of the boys to put away neglected paint brushes and watched the procedure as she helped in the general cleanup. When everything was put away, the two Girl Scouts proceeded to teach their song to the others. They made several mistakes and were convulsed with giggles before they finished. Miss Johnson and the others laughed with them and at them, but no one seemed to mind. The girls tried again without much more success, so Miss Johnson came to their rescue and suggested that with more practice the class would do better. She asked the girls to lead the class in singing a more familiar song. This time the group sang with enthusiasm, obviously enjoying themselves. Even the boys sang heartily, apparently without embarrassment or self-consciousness.

Just then the bell rang and the class was over. The students walked out leisurely, some calling good-bye to Miss Johnson, others jostling each other good-naturedly. A group of three put chairs and tables in order and put away stray books. One or two others remained behind to visit together, and several were talking to Miss Johnson. As Mr. Adams walked over to her, his mind was full of questions. He had seen this class in action, had observed the students' independence, had watched them operate without constant supervision by the teacher. How did these students arrive at this effective level of behavior? How did all of this come about?

CHAPTER 3

Getting Acquainted

As the teacher faces a new class, she has many interpersonal relationships to consider and barriers to break down, many days and months of effort in establishing the "we" feeling that an effective class should have. Until the class learns to plan and evaluate its work, to think through its own problems, the teacher must be the motivating personality. At the same time she must be alert to the other sources of leadership, which are often stronger than her own.

LEARNING NAMES

A feeling of friendliness will eventually result in a class if the teacher is friendly and makes opportunities for the children to become so. One of the first things to do is to learn everyone's name. One cannot work effectively with people one does not know. There are many devices a resourceful teacher may use. Of course, she introduces herself and tells something of her own interests. That may open the way for the students to do the same. Perhaps the first class period or two are spent in this way. Teachers unaccustomed to involving pupils in the planning may feel some insecurity in such time-consuming activities. We have found that the time used thus at the beginning helps students in making adjustments to new class situations. When people talk together, laugh together, and accept one another, they find working together more productive.

Another plan, which is especially good with adolescents who often feel somewhat self-conscious in talking about themselves, is to have students interview each other by twos and introduce each other to the class. This often helps to start a friendly feeling between students who have heretofore not known each other; and the class enjoys making the introductions.

Occasionally classes have been together for some semesters

before and announce that they already know one another well enough. It is usually true that small groups know each other and consider that sufficient; possibly several small cliques already exist. Clique relationships may sometimes be used to advantage, as will be shown in a later chapter, but pupils must learn that each individual is important in the whole group and that knowing just a few will not establish a good working atmosphere. One class had a series of interviews under the heading of "Little Known Facts About Well-Known People." They enjoyed these interviews so much that it was decided to tape-record them. The result was delightful. Many childhood experiences were related. Some students had famous relatives; others had had hair-raising experiences. The whole activity required about three days, but all had such fun that they did not realize they were having a valuable speaking experience that would make speaking before the class, and indeed any group, easier in the future. Better yet, they all looked at one another with new interest and appreciation. The teacher will benefit by entering into such activities, for the class then begins to recognize the teacher's sincerity in wishing to be a real friend to her students.

A memory game is as helpful to the teacher in learning new names as it is to the class. The first person stands and gives his name; the second does the same, adding the name of the first; the third gives his name and the two preceding. When the whole class has participated, everyone's name has been repeated innumerable times, every person has looked every other person smilingly in the face, and the ice is broken. The teacher, who always feels bewildered at the thought of so many strange names to learn, finds that hurdle passed, and she has established in her class a beginning of the group feeling.

Some classes may wish to wear name tags for a few days. Another plan is to make a seating chart on the board for all to copy. A simple technique that provides entertainment and stimulates interest in learning names is to have each pupil make a place card for himself. A page of notebook paper folded in half lengthwise with the pupil's name printed on it with a brush pen can be placed over the edge of his table or desk so that everyone can see it. Students then quickly associate the name with the person in that place.

Learning names can be turned into a spelling lesson, too. Each pupil can make his own spelling list containing the names of the teacher and all the other members of the group. With one or two practices the spelling and pronunciation of all the names are mastered. A final lesson will show that the students can spell and pronounce everyone's name.

The teacher sometimes has to insist on this emphasis on learning names. It is an important requirement, for it attaches importance to each student. No student will function at his best unless he has a sense of his own value in the group.

THE TEACHER'S METHODS OF GETTING ACQUAINTED

Meantime the teacher is collecting information about each student for her own use. If some students present adjustment problems, noticeable perhaps through aggressive or withdrawing behavior, she may begin a series of anecdotal records,[1] which will help her to recognize behavior patterns and eventually to adjust the student to his problems. Students have been asked to write a "get-acquainted" paper, in which they relate some things about themselves: hobbies, interests, spare-time activities, family activities, problems, peeves, travel experiences, or any other revealing factual or interpretive information. This gives the teacher some insight into the writing ability of her students as well as a wealth of miscellaneous information.

The California Test of Personality[2] is a valuable device for information in the fields of personal and social adjustment. Often one problem appears in common with a whole group of students—for example, they may have high social standards but low social skills. Group experience in a class can be valuable in solving this type of problem. Perhaps a few in the class have withdrawing tendencies or a sense of inferior worth. The teacher can use such information in helping the class to organize groups, putting the children who have such problems carefully into groups where they will not feel too inferior or where they can work with a leader who gives them a degree of security.

A teacher can work much more effectively with students if she recognizes and studies the social relationships, the social climate, of the classroom. Early in the year when it is possible to engage in some simple activity using small groups, the teacher can ask, "Who are the best leaders in the class?" Perhaps the whole class will participate in choosing five or six leaders whom they are willing to follow. These leaders in turn can choose or draw names for their groups. Usually, the leaders would rather draw names and then adjust them into effective working groups.

As the teacher spots discipline or adjustment problems in the groups, she can talk over the problems with the leaders. Usually, she does not need to point out the problem possibilities. She gets the leaders together for a short meeting, perhaps while the rest of

[1] See *Helping Teachers to Understand Children*, American Council on Education, Washington, D.C., 1945, for a thorough discussion on anecdotal records.

[2] California Test of Personality, California Test Bureau, 5916 Hollywood Blvd., Los Angeles, California.

the class is doing some written work, and asks them if they need help or would like to talk over any group problems. They have problems aplenty after their first group meetings. Sometimes a complaint will be voiced against one group member. The teacher indicates that the problem member needs a good deal of help, that the leader has been chosen by the others because they are willing to accept his help and judgment, and that the problem member will probably accept the right kind of suggestions from the leader. It is also suggested that problems be talked over in the groups whenever possible. Often a group will call the teacher in to help in the discussion, or a leader may ask the teacher to discuss the problem with a group member. Then the leaders at least are beginning to assume some responsibility for the class. They and others are leraning some of the problems of leadership, and the teacher is learning more about the interpersonal relations in her classroom.

As soon as class members have had an opportunity to get acquainted, a questionnaire upon which to base a sociogram is very helpful to the teacher. Two kinds are useful: the friendship sociogram and the work sociogram. The teacher will need to establish good rapport with her class, as well as to have class members become acquainted with one another, before using this questionnaire. One way is to explain to the class that some information is desired to help the teacher to understand and work better with her students, and then simply to ask the questions: "Who are your best friends in the class?" and "Who are those you would like least for friends?" If a work-relationship chart is desired, the teacher may ask: "Whom do you like best to work with?" and "Whom do you like least to work with?" The students understand that this information is confidential and usually do not object to answering the questions. Sometimes a teacher prefers to imbed these personal questions in a questionnaire that will divulge some other information at the same time. The following one has been used with success:

Name _____ Age___ yrs.___mos.___Date _____

(Answers to these questions are confidential. They will help me to know you better and to do better work with the class. Please answer completely.)

1. Number of members in your family_____. (Include yourself.)
2. Your place in the family (oldest, youngest, etc.)_____.
3. Approximate numbers of hours a day watching TV_____, listening to radio____, reading _____ , doing housework ____, playing outdoors_____.
4. How many movies do you see a week?_____.
5. Do you go to church_____ or Sunday School _____?
6. Other activities that take up your time _____.

In a class like ours your relationships with your classmates are very important. Here is a list of people in the class. Answer the questions about them.

Georgia A.	Bill G.	Pat L.	Doug S.	Bob T.
Ann B.	Larry H.	Karen M.	Jim S.	Richard T.
Don B.	Laura H.	Ray P.	Nancy S.	Ray V.
Carol B.	Carol H.	Eileen R.	John St. A.	Denis W.

1. Who are your best friends or those you would like best to have for friends in this class?

   _____

2. Who are those in the class with whom you would be least likely to make friends?

   _____

3. Who are the ones with whom you like to work best?

   _____

4. Which persons have contributed the most to make the class a success?

   _____

5. What person in the class do you think you could help with his or her problems? How?

   _____

The device of putting the class names on such a questionnaire is very helpful, for then the students are saved the embarrassment of looking somewhat surreptitiously around the room to find answers to the questions.

Information from the sociogram material is used daily. The teacher discovers the leaders, rejects, isolates, mutual dislikes, cliques, and friendship-work parallels. All of this information can be used to help work groups to organize, individuals to become better adjusted, and the isolates and rejects to be brought in casually. All of this cannot be done in a day. It will take time, patience, and self-effacement on the part of the teacher. Obvious handling of such delicate interpersonal relationships is sometimes worse than doing nothing at all. A student who shows good adjustment on the California test, an acceptance by his group in the sociograms, and self-confidence in his everyday actions probably does not have insecurity problems that make it impossible for him to accept someone whom no one else in the class accepts. Thus, the teacher might enlist his help by asking him to do some small bit of work with the isolate. Sometimes the teacher gets a group of accepted children together and asks them what problems they have noticed in the class and what solutions they have to suggest.[3]

---

[3] For further information on sociograms, see *Helping Teachers to Understand Children*.

Chapter 7 will deal in some detail with this method of solving group problems and individual emotional problems.

As the work of the class progresses, the teacher is alert to other bits of information about her students. She soon learns who has special talents and interests, such as artistic ability, manual skill, interesting collections. She learns to use resources from the homes of various students and knows which ones have enriching out-of-school experiences and which have a relatively meager home background. She learns that she must play the mother role to some of the insecure, and that she must not impinge upon the independence of others who are fighting for their place among their peers and who feel that too close a relationship with the teacher will weaken their status with the others. Usually, however, as class work advances and group spirit begins to emerge, the teacher becomes accepted as a working member of the class. The pupil-teacher experiences of the past are important factors in pupil attitudes toward teachers, and sometimes months of patient work are necessary on the part of the teacher to break down predetermined barriers between her and these young people.

Many informal opportunities present themselves to help the teacher get acquainted. Talking casually to students between periods, telling them amusing little personal experiences, laughing together over jokes or puzzles, playing games—these are opportunities not to be missed. There are many opportunities both in and out of the classroom for establishing that important "we" feeling between pupils and teacher and pupils and pupils. In a class where teacher-pupil planning techniques are being used, the teacher must make use of every possible device to build up this attitude. Singing together is fun; some classes like to start their day together with a song. People who laugh, play, sing, and joke together will discover that it is also fun to work together. Pupils who discover that the teacher likes to have fun too do not find it necessary to "put anything over on her."

OTHER SOURCES OF INFORMATION

Most schools have standard information available for all students. Results of mental tests, reading ability scores, health records, attendance records, scholastic records—all of these areas of information are valuable to the teacher in understanding the whole child. Such areas have been more emphasized in the past and therefore are not stressed here as much as the more personal information.

No teacher has the time to make a clinical analysis of every child in her classes. As she begins to gather information, the pupils are at the same time becoming more concerned for one another. As they move further into teacher-pupil planning processes together, the teacher's problems are shared by the class members, and solutions are reached in a cooperative spirit.

LEARNING ABOUT SCHOOL AND ROOM RESOURCES

Another aspect of getting acquainted is that of learning about the resources of the room and the school. The thoughtful teacher can save her pupils many shy and frightened moments, especially in the case of those new to the school, if she creates opportunities for learning the location of various building facilities, such as lavatories, counselor's office, principal's office, library, and other special rooms. Inviting certain key people of the school to visit the class for a few minutes to answer questions or just to say "hello" will help in this phase of orientation: the administrators, the student organization president, the football captain, to suggest a few. Later, the walls of the classroom will also expand into the community, and these first experiences at getting acquainted will help pupils to overcome shyness and to recognize valuable resources, human and otherwise.

SUMMARY

In summary, we emphasize the following points:

1. A feeling of belonging and of class friendliness must be established to make teacher-pupil planning possible. The get-acquainted period is time well spent, and the teacher should feel no anxiety about apparent lack of academic achievement during this time.
2. The teacher must assume the leadership at first and take an active part in all activities for becoming acquainted. Some of these might be:
   a. Teacher introduces self.
   b. Students interview and introduce one another.
   c. Everyone participates in playing memory games, making seating charts, and learning to spell names of fellow students.
3. The teacher will search constantly for means of knowing her pupils better. She will find help from:
   a. Anecdotal records.
   b. Sociometric materials.
   c. California Test of Personality.
   d. Self-made questionnaires.

      e. Informal pieces of writing.

      f. Informal contacts.

      g. School records.

4. The teacher begins as soon as possible to use the leadership ability and other unique abilities of her students to solve the problems of the class and to orient them to the teacher-pupil planning process.

5. Students often have to be urged to become acquainted with one another.

6. Students should be guided in becoming acquainted with the resources of the school—human and material.

CHAPTER 4

Beginnings in Planning

What can a teacher do to accomplish the difficult feat of starting a group on its way to purposeful planning and action? What does she say to her class? What are the first steps to be taken? In the answers to these questions we often find the difference between success and failure in planning with children. The beginnings are all-important. The first day of real planning, organizing for action, sets the stage for future attitudes and behavior toward the teacher, toward classmates, and toward the entire philosophy of planning and working together.

Of course there are as many ways of beginning as there are teachers involved. One learns by doing, and a teacher who is sensitive to the reactions of children and willing to try planning with them can easily find methods for beginning that will suit her purposes and the situation in which she finds herself. In talking with many teachers who want to try planning with students, we find one request almost invariably forthcoming: "Tell us what we should do the first day. Describe an actual class for us." This is most difficult to do since so much depends upon the situation, the group, the teacher, and countless other factors. Here, however, we might present a picture of a group, a teacher, and a setting for the sake of illustrating possible methods for beginnings in planning.

Assuming that the class has become fairly well acquainted with one another and that the teacher knows the names of the students as well as some facts about their previous experiences and backgrounds as described in the preceding chapter, we might proceed in this way:

SETTING: A seventh grade class in English-social studies. The children have had some limited experience with teacher-pupil planning. There is no designated course of study to be followed.

TEACHER (sitting in circle with group): Today we are going to begin planning some activities we might carry out during the time we are together. You know in this class you are going to help me to decide what we shall work on and how we shall go about our work. I am not going to tell you each day that certain things must be done as we go along, but rather we are going to decide together what would be best and most interesting for all of us. In other words, we will all share in the planning of our work. Let's suppose that this is a club that is meeting together for the first time. What might be the first step the club members would take to get their work under way?

STUDENT: Well, in our citizenship club in the sixth grade we had officers. We chose a president and a treasurer and some others to take charge of things.

TEACHER: I see. And do you think that is a good way to run a club?

STUDENT: Yes, I do. It gives the kids a chance to run things by themselves.

TEACHER: What do the rest of you think of Stanley's idea? Would you like to elect officers in this group and operate somewhat as a club might operate?

(General consensus follows through the medium of low mumbling of approval, nodding of heads, etc.)

TEACHER: Suppose we begin, then, by electing a president or chairman. When we have chosen him we can decide whether we will need other officers and how we should go about electing them. What are some of the rules for electing a person to an office?

(A discussion follows that brings out procedures for nominating and voting as well as a review of the qualifications necessary for holding such an office. This discussion is, of course, superficial at this time, going only so far as necessary to facilitate the election at hand. Much is to follow.)

TEACHER: How would it be if I would write the names of the nominees on the board so that no one will be left out this time. Then some one can come up and write down the number of votes as they are counted.

(The election proceeds.)

THE TEACHER'S TECHNIQUES

Notice first that the teacher sits in the circle with the group. Regardless of how the room is arranged, it is desirable for her to make herself and the pupils comfortable by sitting down with them, not taking that time-honored position on her feet in front of the group. Her opening talk is actually noncommittal. She states that the work of the group is to begin with the planning together of some activities they feel they need and want. She makes it clear that she is not going to be the one to make all the decisions, but that everyone will have a share in making them. She stresses the fact that teacher and pupils will work together, thus placing herself as a member of the group. She does not present to the pupils a method for planning by saying, "The majority shall rule" or "You are free to do as you please, so plan somthing you'd like to do." Instead she suggests that they pretend to be a group interested in organizing as a club and then asks the pupils how they could proceed. Acting upon their suggestions, she then assumes the responsibility for getting things under way.

One might say that the teacher is playing too dominant a role in this brief scene, but remember that it is the teacher's direct responsibility to make a good, constructive beginning. She cannot be indecisive at this crucial point; even if it means snatching at straws in the wind, she needs to grasp each idea and carry the class along. In future planning sessions when the group is more skillful in making plans and more ready to offer alternative ideas, her leadership will be less obvious.

A ninth grade class such as the one described in the Preface started planning in this way: The class is acquainted at least superficially, and the atmosphere is somewhat less strained than at first. The teacher guides the thinking of the group thus:

TEACHER: We have three subjects that we are going to study this semester together, and although we know that the things we do are to be within these subjects, perhaps there are things we can do that will be of the most value to all of us. Perhaps you will find that you can help with the planning of what we do, more than you ever have in your one-hour classes. First of all, could we think together for today about what we expect and wish we could get from this class? You have had English classes in the past. What more would you like to get from your English class? Why do we study English anyway?

BOB: To learn grammar; to learn how to diagram sentences.

TEACHER: That is one thing you have done, certainly. (Writes "Grammar" on the board.) What other things might you get from an English class?

THERESA: We learn to write. I would like to be able to write better letters to my friends.

ELAINE: So would I, and sometimes we might have to write business letters, too.

TEACHER: That is a good suggestion. How many of you feel that there might be some value in learning to write different kinds of letters?

(A few students raise their hands and the teacher writes "Letters" on the board. Seeing that a few are beginning to copy the list, she asks if some of them would like to be responsible for an accurate copy, and also if someone will take charge of the list on the board. This releases the teacher to sit more casually with the group, in one of the seats vacated by those who are working at the board. It also relieves most of the students of the necessity of making a list, so that they can give their full thought to the discussion at hand.)

For the most part the suggestions for an English class are rather stereotyped until the teacher points out that all of the suggestions have to do with communication. Students then begin to suggest that they would like to know better how to talk to strangers of their own age, how to introduce people, how to feel at ease with older people, and how to get over nervousness when talking. The students are much more responsive to these ideas than to the suggestions about grammar. Other suggestions, such as becoming acquainted with different kinds of reading or knowing about poetry, are also greeted with approval, and the list is growing.

TEACHER: Some of your suggestions here seem to indicate that you would like to do many things that will help you to get over your self-consciousness. The study of social living was added to our curriculum for exactly that reason. Since all of you have chosen social living as your elective subject this year, just what did you hope to get from it?

BETTY: I heard they had parties and learned how to act.

TOM: I heard they learned about business meetings.

TEACHER: Those are practical things to learn, aren't they? What are some of the other things a course like this might help you with?

BARBARA: Well, I don't know whether this is right or not, but I think we ought to learn something about how to get along together in school and at home and maybe in the world.

TEACHER: That might solve many of our problems if we could learn a valuable lesson like that.

The discussion continues, with the teacher making sure that every idea is brought out and everyone who has any idea is recognized. She and the others help the writers to list the ideas. A discussion of the civics course brings out a desire to know how the city is run, what communism is, how political parties are organized, and other similar suggestions. This discussion will take a full hour and possibly will be resumed after a break.

With all the ideas on the board, the teacher then asks if anyone sees some that might be combined under a single heading. Many suggestions are made, and the students are given a practical experience in outlining. This process would become tiring, however, if continued indefinitely, and the teacher asks if a few would like to meet with her and finish the outline so that everyone can have a copy. Time is allowed in the next morning's schedule, and a copy of the result is put into every student's hands and filed in his notebook for frequent future reference. Thus the initial planning period has a practical use, and as the class progresses each student feels that he has had a part in what is being done.

Another technique that some teachers like to use is to spend time with their groups discussing various ways that the class might be operated. They hear every member's viewpoint and then make their decisions as to how the class shall be run. It is well to insert a word of warning here. Many teachers have spent hours discussing with their groups the desirability of having the students help in planning. Upon occasion they have met with the students' absolute refusal to accept this method of operation because some of them may have had an unprofitable, unhappy experience with it in previous years. In most instances it is better for the teacher to state generally that the class will operate on a cooperative, sharing basis, and thus avoid any unpleasantness that may follow. A discussion of possible methods of operation is helpful if the group is experienced in several methods and mature enough to judge their merits. If handled well by the teacher it can be most profitable, but it does present problems that should be carefully considered before beginning.

All of these methods for beginning planning with pupils have their merits, some more than others, of course. There is danger in allowing students too much freedom at the very beginning and there is danger in allowing the teacher to dominate the situation. A happy medium must be reached, depending upon many factors: the group with which the teacher is working, the previous experience of the group and its maturity level, the subject matter boundaries, school policies, and community pressures, to mention only a few.

SELECTING TOPICS FOR STUDY

We have looked in on two types of beginning planning sessions. In one we saw the planning start with the organization of the class into a kind of club. In the other we saw the planning begin with suggestions from the students relative to their desired expectations for the year. Let us look now at a situation where a free choice of subject matter is allowed, keeping more or less within the boundaries of two courses, English and social studies. After the group has been organized to a degree, we ask ourselves the logical question, "Where do we go from here? What are the next steps?"

Suppose that another class session is at hand. It is time to begin selecting topics for study. The teacher might begin by saying: "We have been given the opportunity to decide what we shall work on this year. We are fortunate in having more time together in this class than you have in any other class. No one is going to tell us we must do a certain number of things, but we may decide what we will work on and how we can proceed. What are some things you would like to learn about and do this year?"

Invariably hands will shoot up. The ice has been broken, ideas have been requested, and the time for action is at hand. Lists of possible topics to study, things to learn about and do, are fascinating to peruse. Ideas spring from the innermost recesses of the minds. Some are fantastic. Some show real curiosity and mature thought. Some are nonsense.

All suggestions can be placed on the list at this time as having equal status regardless of their worth. A teacher who is wise will not reject any topic, because it is at this point that some pupils will try her out to prove to themselves whether she means what she has said about their choosing what they can work on. Some seemingly silly topics may be suggested, but rarely should any be discarded initially. In making this list the teacher can submit suggestions of her own. Her ideas need not be elaborated upon, but one or two topics that she states can be included just as the students' topics are included.

The variety of the students' selections and the significance of the topics is impressive. It is indicative of the real concerns of pupils and their ability to reason and plan if given the opportunity.

How do we sort them? How do we make this jumbled list a meaningful program for a year's work? (See Sample A.)

Sample A

TEMPORARY LIST OF TOPICS TO STUDY

7 - I's

First Semester, 196—

I. The United Nations
    A. Membership and organization
    B. History
    C. Function

II. Conservation
    A. Trees
    B. Animals
    C. Land
    D. Natural resources of all kinds

III. Safety and Health
    A. Common diseases
    B. History of medicine
    C. Sanitation
    D. Why practice safety?
    E. How can safety rules be practiced?
    F. New medicines
    G. How can we follow health rules?

IV. National Defense
    A. New weapons of the United States
    B. Universal Military Training
    C. The A-bomb
    D. The H-bomb
    E. Cost of defense

V. Personal Problems
   A. How to overcome shyness
   B. Sisters and brothers
   C. School and teachers
   D. Personal appearance
   E. How to be popular

VI. Our High School
   A. Clubs
   B. Teachers
   C. Subjects
   D. Extra subjects
   E. The administration
   F. The building
   G. Our teams
   H. History

VII. Crime in the United States
   A. Juvenile delinquency
   B. Prevention
   C. Causes
   D. Police departments
   E. How to solve crimes

VIII. History and Government of the United States
   A. Wars of the United States
   B. How does our government work?
   C. Early settlers
   D. Relations with other countries

IX. Racial and Religious Prejudice
   A. Religions of the world
   B. Negroes in the United States
   C. Why are Jews persecuted?

X. Leisure Time Activities
   A. Sports for boys
   B. Sports for girls
   C. Movies
   D. Radio
   E. Television
   F. Good reading
   G. Comic books
   H. Hobbies

SETTING UP GOALS

After a temporary list of topics has been suggested, it is only logical to stop and consider with students the goals that they and the teacher have in mind for the coming year. The question can be put to them somewhat in this manner: "We've made a list now of things we'd like to study and do this year. Before we do any more with our list, let's ask ourselves these questions: What are our reasons for suggesting these topics? What are some of the goals that we have in mind for ourselves? What are some things we want to accomplish?"

Some of the students may not have any goals in mind or may need to have the idea of reaching predetermined goals explained to them more fully. But after a few ideas have been put on the board, more will come, and soon a list of goals to strive for is in the making. This list need not be a finished product at first, but rather should point the way toward choosing worthwhile activities that will help students to achieve their goals. It can be changed from time to time. Additions will need to be made and perhaps some of the goals will be deleted as the group matures in its thinking. A list of goals for a year's work can be found in Samples B and C.

Sample B

GOALS FOR THE YEAR

7 - 3's

We of the 7-3's want to accomplish these things this year:

1. To get good marks
2. To pass to eighth grade
3. To make friends and be good sports
4. To get along with the teacher
5. To learn to work cooperatively
6. To improve in writing down our thoughts
7. To learn to speak better before a group
8. To improve in reading aloud
9. To learn to understand what we read
10. To learn about the problems other people have all over the world
11. To improve personal habits and appearance
12. To learn to use the library
13. To learn about our school and be active
14. To study hard and really learn
15. To improve our grammar
16. To keep the room looking nice
17. To obey all rules and behave ourselves
18. To think before we speak and act
19. To improve our penmanship

Sample C

9B GENERAL EDUCATION

September, 196_

Our expectations of what we may learn in English, civics, and social living:

I. Getting Along Better with People
   A. How to act in a group
   B. How to develop good manners for parties and other occasions

C. How to start a conversation
D. How to make friends
E. Learning about people and their problems

II. Communicating Effectively
  A. Writing
    1. Themes   3. Business letters
    2. Letters   4. Book reports
  B. Speaking
    1. Get over nervousness   4. Pronounce words clearly
    2. Use good English   5. Make conversation
    3. Express ourselves   interesting
       well   6. Learn to introduce people
  C. Listening
    1. Be courteous   2. Learn from listening
  D. Reading
    1. Read better, both orally and silently
    2. Enjoy all sorts of poetry
    3. Know what words mean
    4. Become acquainted with good literature

III. Understanding Government
  A. What is the difference between the two big political parties?
  B. Why do we have government?
  C. What is our relationship with other countries and other
    forms of government?
  D. What is communism? How does it differ from our form of
    government?
  E. Learn about our national government
    1. Congress
    2. How is government financed?
    3. Who are the chief government officials?
  F. Learn about the government of our state
  G. Learn about the government of our city
  H. Find out what we ourselves can do about world affairs

IV. Learning How to Study
  A. Thinking clearly and effectively
  B. Enjoying our work
  C. Using our time wisely

Now we are ready for the next step. The pupils have their lists of the topics they suggested. Perhaps a student committee has refined and organized the list since the class first made it. This committee can report on its work at this time, putting the revised list on the board for the others to copy. Or the teacher may have done this work herself and be ready to give each member of the group a dittoed copy for his notebook. The organization of topics can be accomplished with the group as a whole, using the activity as a lesson in outlining. In any case a more organized list is developed. All of the original suggestions are there, but some classifying has been done to make the list more usable.

Where do we begin? What shall we work on first? Everyone is eager to have his pet topic chosen by the group. Several boys want "football and other sports" and nothing else! The girls want to work on "fashions through the ages." One pupil wants to work only on "Michigan." How can we decide? Here the teacher needs to explain carefully that the class will try to cover all the topics at some time during the year and that everyone will have a chance to do the thing he particularly wants to do if at all possible. She can appeal to the good sportsmanship of all the pupils and suggest that the best way to proceed is to try to decide together just where to begin. Then she can move on and suggest that the class vote on all the topics and see which which five topics receive the greatest number of votes.

CRITERIA FOR SELECTING A TOPIC

The vote is taken and five topics that are favored at the moment are selected. Let us look at these suggestions. Let us consider for a moment, "What should a topic do for us if we are going to spend our time on it?" In other words, what are the criteria for selecting a topic for study?

This step is most important. In stating some criteria for selecting a topic we assure ourselves that our time will be well spent. A topic must meet the criteria set up or it will not be considered. Pupils are honest enough to consider this seriously and they will not often make unwise decisions. Once they have made rules for themselves they follow those rules. The teacher needs only to remind them of the criteria or rules before the final choice is made. Even if a topic cannot meet every qualification, the mere process of considering its merit is invaluable. At any rate the decision is not irrevocable, and if and when mistakes are made, they can be remedied without undue concern. Sample D is a list of criteria for selecting a topic to study as set by a seventh grade group.

Now we are ready for the final voting. We have organized our list of topics and we have set up criteria for choosing a topic. The choice has been narrowed to five main items. A teacher can use any of several methods here to determine which topic will be chosen. Sometimes it is better for the pupils to vote for just one—the one they want most to work on as a beginning topic. Or perhaps the teacher may ask them to vote for three topics and go on from there to single out one, using a variety of voting schemes. As long as the students keep the criteria in mind and make a sincere effort to choose a worthwhile topic, the choice can be made fairly easily.

Sample D

RULES FOR CHOOSING A TOPIC

7-1's

196_ - 196_

1. The topic should be one that we have not studied before.
2. The topic should be one that will help us now and later in life.
3. The topic should be one that is interesting to almost everyone in the class.
4. The topic should be one that will give us practice in reading, writing, using the library, working together, and speaking.
5. The topic should be important and serious. We should know when we get through that what we have studied is valuable.
6. The topic should be one on which there is sufficient information for us to use in our study.
7. The topic should increase our knowledge.

BREAKING DOWN A TOPIC

The next question teachers will ask is, "How does one satisfy the minority group?" or "What happens if the class can't decide upon any one topic?" or "Can the group work on more than one topic at a time?"

Again the answers to these questions are to be found in the situation. It is difficult many times to bring a group to a point where all members are interested in a sole activity. However, there are many phases to each activity, and when opposition to the choice of the group arises, the skillful teacher can point out to the dissenters how they might work on some phase of the topic that will interest and challenge them. There is a place for everyone in each activity even though it is sometimes difficult to find.

How do we break down a topic that the group has chosen so that every member of the group can participate in the study? A good way to begin is to find a meaningful title for the topic. Putting the title into question form turns it into a problem to be solved instead of simply an area of study. For example, if students have chosen to study Egypt they might state the problem like this: "What is modern Egypt like?" or "What does Egypt contribute to the world today?" One group chose to work on "wars of the United States" and after considerable discussion they decided to entitle their study "What has the United States gained by warfare?" In this way, all of the various phases of the topic can be investigated and questioned. All groups can focus their work on the answer to one problem, and many facets will be brought together at the end of the study for meaningful discussion relative to the solution of that problem.

Here are several techniques that can be used with students to break down a topic and to find areas in which each group member can participate:

1. The group can be numbered off at random so that several smaller groups of five or six are organized. The teacher might ask the groups to meet for ten or fifteen minutes and to make a list of about ten questions they want answered relative to the chosen topic. She can appoint a chairman and a recorder for each group and point out the location in the room where each group will meet. Following the meetings, the groups can report their questions to the entire class. The teacher can write them on the board or collect them later and either assign a committee to organize the list or organize it herself. The finished list will be a guide that will help to organize the small working groups. Each pupil may choose the phase of the topic that interests him most. Some may have to make a second choice if one phase of the topic proves to be enticing to too large a group, but this can be accomplished amicably if the teacher uses ingenuity.

2. It may be that the class is not ready to go into small groups, but handles itself well in a general discussion session. If this is the case, it is fairly easy to pose the question "What do we want to find out about this topic we've chosen?" As the suggestions come from the group they can be written on the board and then organized into a working outline. Each student may choose the phase he wants to work on. Some parts of the outline may not appeal to anyone. These can be placed in reserve in the event one group completes its work far before the others and needs extra work.

3. Each student in the class might be assigned the task of writing down a series of questions related to the selected topic. If the teacher is expected to assign homework, this can be a part of it. Parents can be brought into the planning in this way. When the class meets again, the list can be read and all the different questions put on the board. If a seat-work type of activity is in order, each pupil can organize the miscellaneous questions for himself, and the main topics can then be listed for the entire class to see.

With this part of the work of teacher-pupil planning, as with all parts, there are many possible techniques to use. There are new methods to discover, old ones to follow, revise, or cast out. One set pattern of operation is obviously out of the question if we want to work with pupils as individual human beings.

Our answer to the question "Can the group work on more than one topic at a time?" is that it is completely possible and can even be highly desirable at a more advanced stage of teacher-pupil planning. However, it does present further complications. It means that the teacher must be doubly alert to the work of the groups, and that the demands upon her for help and resources are widely diversified. When the group becomes more skillful in the techniques of group work they can proceed better on their own, but they need a great deal of help from the teacher in the beginning stages. For these reasons it is perhaps more advisable to keep the group together at first. This serves to safeguard the peace of mind of both the pupils and the teacher.

THE TIME ELEMENT IN PLANNING

Let us pause for a moment to consider the time element at this stage of our teacher-pupil planning. Have all these steps been taken in one or two days? Indeed not. We are, perhaps, in the third or fourth week of the school year, depending upon how much time was needed to bring the class to a point where they were ready to plan.

Children lose interest in any activity when it is prolonged. Planning together can become uninteresting too if we spend too much time on it. A good way to avoid this is to vary the day's activities as much as possible. An hour or half an hour of a class session each day in planning together is ample time at first. Then the teacher can assign other work she feels the class might profit by until its plans are actually under way.

She might want to learn just where her class stands in reading ability. If office records cannot supply her with this information, reading tests can be administered. Perhaps the students can do some writing to illustrate their capabilities in that area. There will be new textbooks to explore, work around the room that needs to be done, orientation trips to the school library that need to be arranged, and countless other activities to fill each day and vary the program. Before many class sessions pass, the teacher will find herself wishing that each group could have just one more hour together.

To illustrate how many things there are to be done in these beginning days, we can look at a seventh grade group that organized itself as a club. The group held a brief meeting each morning at the beginning of class. The president called the group to order, the secretary took the roll. Following this, the president asked for any business that needed to come before the group. Out of one of these discussions came the suggestion that it might be a good idea to form a committee to beautify the room. (The teacher had deliberately done nothing in the classroom in the way of decorations or displays.) After many suggestions were made as to what could be done, a committee was formed. In a day or two the committee presented its report. It was suggested that plastic draperies would add a great deal to the attractiveness of the room. The class accepted this suggestion with enthusiasm and began planning how the necessary funds could be raised, how the draperies could be hung, how they were to be purchased, and countless other small details.

Needless to say, this plan took time, but within a few weeks (with the help of the teacher, the home economics teacher, and the janitor) colorful plastic draperies graced the long windows. For the remainder of the year the students proudly displayed the results of their efforts to anyone who would take the time to look. This activity was only the beginning, and subsequent projects not only produced many attractive and useful things for the room but also served to create a friendly, cooperative spirit and a feeling of oneness in the group. The room and all the things in it belonged to the class. All had had a part in making it a pleasant place to be in, and they felt that it was their responsibility to keep it looking cheerful.

TECHNIQUES FOR TEACHING GROUP WORK

Now comes the crucial moment when actual work on the projects begins. All the preliminaries are arranged and the small working groups are ready to meet. What happens? It is possible that everything will go smoothly. The groups may contain leaders with enough ability to carry the others along and help them to proceed with their work quite independently. They may have had enough experience with group work to be able to organize and move ahead without too much help. This situation would, of course, be nothing short of utopian; more often than not the teacher finds quite the opposite occurring.

We often err in taking for granted the native ability of people to work together harmoniously. Adults are frequently heard complaining about the abilities of committee members to function effectively. Time is wasted in idle chatter, issues are evaded or overlooked, some members dominate the discussion, some contribute nothing, the chairman is a weakling—all are common complaints. If this takes place in adult groups, how then can we expect children to know innately how to function in a small group? We cannot. We have to teach them how. "But won't they learn by doing?" you ask. Yes, that is the only way they will learn, but a helping hand from the teacher pointing out pitfalls and offering constructive suggestions for improvement proves invaluable in the process.

A teacher cannot anticipate each mistake her students will make. She cannot expect group work to run smoothly at first. Students will need help as they advance with their work, even with such a simple task as shifting from the general circle into smaller groups. Making sure that groups know where they are to meet and what they are to do facilitates moving around the room and settling down to work.

When pupils are working in small groups the teacher is afforded one of her best opportunities to work with her students. She can visit each group for a brief time just listening or inserting a word or two here and there. In that way she directs the pupils' endeavors toward more constructive ends. In time her students will feel comfortable when she sits in with a group and will welcome her help and approval, not as one who sits in only to criticize negatively but as an interested, concerned group member. The teacher who views the time when small groups are working as an opportunity to catch up on work at her desk or to run off on an errand will find that her groups do not produce nearly the amount of work she expects.

In addition to visiting the groups, the teacher will want to hear from each group from time to time so that she can be sure the work is progressing. Progress reports from the groups are interesting and sometimes stimulating to other pupils, too. Some teachers like to hear briefly from the chairman of each group before the group meetings begin. Then if there are suggestions from the teacher or class about how the group could improve its work, they can be made before the day's meeting begins. Some teachers prefer to hear from the groups after they have been working on their projects. This technique is a good way to tie up loose ends and make constructive plans for the next working session.

Teachers are using with success a variety of written forms to keep tabs on the work of small groups. These are effective because they give students an opportunity to organize their plans and accomplishments in writing. The written report also allows the teacher to comment in writing on the progress of each pupil, thus evaluating his work and supplying suggestions for improvement. Some of the many written forms that can be used are illustrated in Samples E and F.

If it is easy to see that there are a great many ways for a teacher to keep in touch with the work of small groups. Whatever methods are used, the teacher will find that this is an essential part of her work. Merely watching her groups does not suffice. She needs to work with them and to know at all times what progress they are

Sample E

PROGRESS REPORT I

   I. What is the problem your group is working on?

  II. What reading materials are you using to obtain information?

 III. In what other ways do you plan to get information?

  IV. How are you getting along in your group?

   V. What plans are you making for your illustrative material?

  VI. What plans are you making to report your findings to the class?

 VII. Do you need help in any way?

Signed _____

Sample F

PROGRESS REPORT II

   I. When does your group plan to report to the class?

  II. How does your group plan to give its report?

 III. What did you do to illustrate your findings?

  IV. Name the books, magazines, pamphlets, and other printed sources that you have used to obtain your information. Tell where you got these materials.

   V. Name any other sources of information you used.

  VI. Do you need more time on this project? If so, tell how much and why.

Signed _____

making. If she makes the effort to do this, she will find that the groups take their work seriously and that wasted time is cut to a minimum.

Illustrative materials help a great deal in showing students how group members can operate effectively. A series of etched glass slides which teachers or students can easily make can be used effectively. Pupils like to look at slides. These can illustrate the duties of the chairman, the recorder, and the group members. Printed comments to accompany each picture or diagram can be made on a typewriter with special cellophane and carbon paper used for this purpose. This kind of device can be put to good use again and again.

A series of beaver-board cards can be used on which are printed such titles as "Slacker," "Idea Man," "Talker," "Good Listener," "Worker," "Slave Driver," or any other designations that seem appropriate. In general class discussion dealing with an evaluation of group work, these can be placed on a blackboard or bulletin board to show how the group looked from the pupils' as well as the teacher's viewpoint.

The sociodrama is an excellent medium for conveying the idea of how small groups work. The teacher might ask several students to assume various roles she has observed being played while the groups were working. The roles can be planned so that an ideal committee meeting is acted out before the group, or they can be planned to illustrate a poor committee meeting. There is a definite therapeutic value in having students who have not been working effectively assume the good or proper roles. By the same token, a student who has been a dominating leader might take the part of a confused member, for example, so that he will feel something of what his less forceful classmate is experiencing. A discussion following the sociodrama can be invaluable in helping the pupils to identify their own behavior patterns and thus improve the effectiveness of group work.

Whatever methods are used, teachers will find that constant evaluation of how groups are proceeding will help in the amount and quality of the work being done. These techniques will be used through the year, since effective participation in group work cannot be mastered during the first week. The problems must be shared by all concerned.

In summarizing this discussion of techniques for teaching group work, there are four basic principles to be followed:

1. Make sure that students know what they are to do when they form small groups. Directions should be explicit, yet limited.
2. Work with the small groups. Circulate among them, listening to their conversations, making suggestions whenever appropriate.
3. Have groups report periodically on their work either in written form or in a general class session.
4. Evaluate with the pupils the work of the groups. Help them to point out good and bad features of their work and behavior.

SUMMARY

In concluding this chapter, we would like to note several major points.

1. The foregoing descriptions of techniques for teacher-pupil planning are only a few of the many techniques that can be employed. Teachers use literally hundreds of different techniques in planning with students. The individual teacher who desires to experiment will accept some methods and reject others. Her own capabilities, the group she is working with, and the situation in which she finds herself will determine the procedures she uses.

2. The early stages of planning are very important. Here the teacher finds herself in a precarious position and she must handle the situation carefully. It is infinitely better to begin planning with pupils on a small scale and then to work out to larger boundaries than to throw the field wide open on the first day. The teacher can then maintain her own security and the pupils will realize that the situation is well controlled.

3. The transition for students from a teacher-dominated classroom to a classroom where teacher-pupil planning takes place is not always made with ease. Students are eager to have a share in planning, for the most part, but because of previous conditioning they may oppose the idea or reject it entirely. Skillful action on the part of the teacher can avoid an unpleasant situation. She needs only to state simply that the class will operate on a cooperative basis and the groundwork is laid. She does not have to place herself in the midst of a controversial issue if she is careful to take all elements of the situation into consideration.

4. The process of choosing a topic to study is fascinating and challenging for both teachers and pupils. Approaching the problem slowly, giving equal importance to each suggestion, classifying the various ideas in a usable outline, and setting up with the students some criteria for choosing a topic for study will all help in making worthwhile choices.

5. Goals for the year as expressed by the students will help to make the selection of topics to study more meaningful. If the students put some thought into the matter of their purposes for the year's work, the work will take on added meaning. They can then focus their work on achieving their goals.

6. Breaking down a topic into smaller areas of study is important because each student needs to find some area in which

he can work. Creating a problem to be solved instead of simply studying a general topic serves to make the information the students compile more meaningful.

7. Too much time spent in planning can create a stumbling block. Students are eager for action but the process cannot be rushed. Varied activities carefully planned for definite purposes can be alternated with planning sessions so that the group does not become restless and bored with the actual planning of the work.

8. Helping students to learn how to work in small groups is an important part of the teacher's work. Pupils will learn these techniques only by experiencing the group process, but the teacher can provide much valuable help as the learning proceeds.

CHAPTER 5

Plans in Action

As students become more skilled in planning and working processes, the projects they participate in will become more complicated. Many interesting activities may be taking place daily either as a part of a major project or as some special or unique interest of the class.

The teacher who has been completely guided by a course of study may feel uncertain at this time that a real academic work unit can ever be followed through to conclusion in a class that does its own planning. In this chapter, therefore, a unit will be followed through all of its various phases. We shall also show planning and working methods in a variety of class activities that might be a part of any class year.

The class described here is in its eighth month of teacher-pupil planning experiences. The unit is a part of a vocations course required of all ninth grade students in the junior high school. Preceding this phase of the work, the class has had a self-analysis unit, in which they have made a rather comprehensive study of personality and character traits, particularly their own. They have worked with numerous questionnaires, the Kuder Interest Inventory,[1] the Purdue Pegboard Test of Manual Dexterity,[2] and various other devices. A brief survey of the family vocational interests for two or three generations has been made by each pupil. Pupils have also been reading biographies in which unique abilities and interests have been noted, and each pupil has written an autobiography. He has also examined his academic record and has had numerous informal conferences with his teacher and his fellow students about his own interests and abilities. A film, *Finding Your Life Work*,[3] was a good introduction to thinking about the individual and his place in the world of work.

---

[1] Kuder Interest Inventory, Science Research Associates, 57 West Grand Ave., Chicago, Illinois.

[2] Purdue Pegboard Test, *ibid.*

[3] *Finding Your Life Work*, Vocational Guidance Films, Carl F. Mahnke Productions; from University of Michigan Audio-Visual Education Center.

A talk by the teacher introduced the idea that all occupations can be classified, for convenience in studying similarities, into nine general fields of work. Since the goal of the standard course in civics for the semester was to study vocations, the class readily agreed on the study of all these fields as a good continuing point. Their choice lay in determining how this unit might be approached, what they hoped to accomplish from it, and how it would fit into their basic goals. Some time before, the following list of goals had been agreed upon:

General Education Class Goals

A. To learn to get along well with others
   1. Work and live better together
   2. Work harmoniously
   3. Be courteous
   4. Show respect for others
   5. Have a feeling of friendliness

B. To improve communication
   1. Learn to talk easily to strangers
   2. Learn to talk without self-consciousness to adults
   3. Increase vocabulary
   4. Write better
   5. Speak easily and better
   6. Use better grammar
   7. Learn to control voice
   8. Learn to listen courteously and intelligently

C. To develop good individual personality
   1. Overcome self-consciousness
   2. Be able to do things for yourself
   3. Develop self-control
   4. Assume responsibility
   5. Be prompt
   6. Analyze yourself
   7. Use common sense and good judgment
   8. Respect property, your own and others'
   9. Show respect for others
   10. Be friendly

D. To achieve an interesting and worthwhile class
   1. Get work done on time
   2. Keep good classroom order
   3. Develop good manners
   4. Develop better working habits
   5. Plan a good course for senior high

6. Encourage everyone to participate
7. Have good discussions
8. Learn to understand, interpret, and discuss the news
9. Plan interesting group projects
10. Work effectively and harmoniously in groups
11. Learn the role of a chairman
12. Learn the role of a recorder and all other group members
13. Encourage and give good oral reports
14. Be where you should at any given time
15. Be familiar with class goals

The class has already divided itself into five working groups of six students each. They preferred—a choice reached by trial and error method throughout the year—to do all small-group work in a group organized for several weeks at a time. They had in their own opinion begun to acquire some skill in working together, and they felt that too frequent disruption of working groups interfered with their progress.

The nine fields of work were examined, and each group made a first and second choice. There was a bit of give and take necessary in this process, as in any group of people where personal preferences are decisive factors. Students who had already made some decision as to their own occupations preferred to study the field in which that one was classified. This plan was obviously impossible for all, and the teacher explained that each student would have a vast amount of source material from the group work to use in making an individual study of an occupation later in the semester.

Finally, the choices were made and the pupils were ready to start examining and collecting material. After two or three days at this task, which took them to the several textbooks in the classroom, a large file collection, and the school library, a general class meeting was held in which they agreed upon a basic set of goals for the project, described later in this chapter. Following this accomplishment, attention was called to a list everyone had previously filed in his notebook of interesting ways in which material could be presented to a group. With the goals and the suggestions for presenting information in mind, the group could continue collecting material and at the same time be thinking of the best way to share it with the rest of the class.

The list of ways of presenting material, as shown below, was compiled after a free class discussion, with thoughtful consideration given to everyone's suggestions.

Ways of Presenting Information

Reports	Glass slides
Panel discussions	Opaque boards
Debates	Bulletin boards
Floor talks	Scrapbooks
Dialogues	Posters
Dramatizations	Booklets
Sociodramas	Film strips
Tape recordings	Flannel board
Radio broadcasts	Mimeographed material
Chalk talks	Charts and diagrams
Quiz programs	Drawings

Each group and each individual in it began to work in unique ways. Some skill had now been developed in finding work that each one could do best, so that the weaker academic students could find a variety of manual and physical tasks to help the group. A two-hour block from the three hours the class met was often set aside by the planning committee at the request of the other pupils so that they could work without interruption. A typical day might find the following activities under way:

The group studying clerical jobs has a nine-thirty appointment with the office manager of one of the large industrial firms. They spend ten or fifteen minutes before leaving in reviewing the questions they have planned for the interview. They ask the teacher to check over the questions to see that they have covered the different items of information they hope to get.

The group studying agriculture is collecting farm pictures, which they expect to show on the opaque projector. Two boys from the group have an appointment with the visual-aids teacher to learn how to use the projector effectively. Another boy is reading and taking notes on some pamphlets on poultry farming, preparatory to getting his report ready for presentation with the pictures. Another girl and boy are cutting out pictures from a number of periodicals that the group members have brought. The other girl in the group is in the library working with some ephemeral material in the files.

The group working on craftsmen and operatives is examining book and file material and planning a field trip to one of the factories. The two boys who have volunteered to do the calling to make arrangements are consulting with the teacher as to what they should say. There is a discussion with this group in which good telephone manners are reviewed, and a brief dramatization of the call as it might be made is given by volunteers. The problem of who is to go on the field trip is also being considered. Should it be just for this group, or is it of broad enough importance to include the whole class?

The groups working on mining, manufacturing, and transportation are preparing talks to be used with the glass slides being made by the artistic members. Two of the boys have decided to preview some film-strips and go to reserve the equipment for the next work period. One member puts a sign on the bulletin board, after consulting with the bulletin board committee, which says "Reserved for Group III."

The group working on professional vocations is listing and sorting out the occupations they hope to cover in their reports. They are planning a scrapbook that will illustrate some of the chief professions, and they also hope to have some dramatizations that will illustrate qualities necessary for success in certain professions.

The teacher, of course, is in constant demand by one group or another. She sits down with them and gives her attention to their problems: in planning, in locating materials, in settling differences.

It will be noted that some time has had to be spent in planning together in order to correlate the activities of all groups. It is a valuable experience for students to plan in this way for they must consider the personal wishes of each one, as well as the values to be gained by the entire class.

When the groups have worked long enough so that they can plan ahead to definite dates, a schedule is set up. Each student is given an outline that includes the goals and schedule agreed upon by the class, nine fields of work outlines on which to take notes when reporting, and an evaluation sheet. This evaluation sheet had been discussed by the class and the work of organizing it delegated to a small committee composed of a member of each group and the teacher. The evaluation is, of course, based on the goals of the project and allows for an academic grade. The fact that the group will rate each individual in terms of his contribution to the project usually acts as a motivating factor to some extent, but the cooperative way of doing the work eliminates the factor of competition, one of the questionable values of our educational grading system.

The plans, outlines, and schedule for presentations and evaluation sheets, all necessary to unify and clarify the work, were in the hands of all students.

Fields of Work

Goals of the Project

    I. To learn what the fields of work are and to acquire some general informtaion about each
       A. Kinds of jobs in each field
       B. Requirements
          1. Educational
            a. Cost

    2. Physical

    3. Special abilities

    4. Work experience

  C. Working conditions

  D. Opportunities

  E. Earnings

II. To learn where I, with my individual interests and abilities, will fit into the world of work

III. To learn where information is

IV. To learn to get information

V. To develop skills in getting along with others

  A. In planning

  B. In sharing information

  C. In cooperating

VI. To get experience in

  A. Reporting information in our own words

  B. Listening

  C. Taking notes

  D. Writing

  E. Using correct grammar

Plans for reaching these goals required research, reading, interviews, and writing. Results were reported to the class by each group and each individual within it. Time was allowed for class questions and discussion and for a group-composed quiz to test the success of the presentation and the listening ability of the class. Finally, each student was responsible for his own evaluation, as follows:

EVALUATION OF FIELDS OF WORK PROJECT   Name _____

(This evaluation is based on the goals of our project. It was planned by a representative from each group, Nancy, Jim, Ann, Bob, Henry, and Miss Barrett. Some of these questions will be your individual evaluation; some of them must be determined by the group. Consider each carefully and fairly.)

A. Learning about the fields of work and my place as a worker

  1. Did I learn what the fields of work are and what some of the representative jobs are in each field? _____

  2. Did I learn about vocations for which I seem to be suited?____

B. Finding and using information

  1. References I read: _____

  2. Interviews I had with people outside of school: _____

C. Developing skills in getting along with others

  1. Did I have information to bring to each group meeting? _____

  2. Did I make suggestions which helped our group planning? ____

  3. Arrangements I made for the group or the class: _____

  4. Did I get along well with my group? _____

5. Did I use group time wisely? _____
6. Was I dependable in doing my share? _____
D. Getting experience in communications skills
   1. How did I help my group to present materials to the class?___
   2. Did I listen courteously and intelligently to group and class reports? _____.
   3. What writing experience did I have? _____
   4. Is my grammar improving? What errors have I overcome?___
E. What grade does my group give me?
   Scholarship _____ Citizenship _____
   Signed _____, Chairman _____, Recorder

As any teacher knows, a ninth grader's span of attention is limited, no matter how fascinating the project. We cannot expect pupils to work continuously on one project, especially in a class scheduled in a block of three hours. The planning committee, through experience, has foreseen this. There are long-term goals to be considered in the total work of the class. While it is unwise to have too many major projects under way at one time, a variety of other activities may be planned.

When the time comes for group projects to be presented, the groups are responsible for all arrangements of physical facilities. They often have to rearrange the furniture for dramatizations or use of visual aids, and the evaluation of this group by the rest of the class is based partly upon the dispatch with which they perform these necessary tasks. The group itself is quick to recognize its mistakes and to learn how to avoid pitfalls. Often a weak group will give a much better report on a second project than on a first, having learned from good presentations to recognize its own weaknesses.

The treatment of a unit in which teacher-pupil planning methods are used is quite different from one that is wholly planned by the teacher. The inclination of the teacher would be to have every pupil study every field of work, with perhaps a few extra projects by individuals or groups. The goals would necessarily be different—that is, the class would probably be expected to learn what the teacher had assigned. Thus, the evaluation would also be different, probably limited to teacher grades on reports, outlines, or notebooks and a teacher-composed examination. We feel that a broader set of goals has been approached in the method described here, and that students, having had the experience of planning their experiences, will have found the whole unit meaningful.

Here in summary are some of the unique experiences the students have had:

1. Telephoning for appointments

2. Meeting people in various kinds of work in the community
3. Writing letters of thanks for favors
4. Interviewing
5. Conducting themselves courteously in public
6. Getting information from many different sources
7. Sharing and planning information with the small group
8. Presenting information with the small group
9. Reading, writing, outlining, taking notes
10. Working amiably and purposefully with others

These experiences took place in addition to the more usual classroom procedures that would be found in the more formal classroom. Does it not seem that a student who had had these experiences would be better able to solve many of the problems of both the young and the adult world?

The teacher notes that a failure in situations where the pupils have done the planning is much more of a learning experience than the same result of a teacher-planned unit. When the students have helped to make the plans, set up the goals, and evaluate the results, their concern with how they could have done better is much more productive than when the teacher has done the whole backgound work alone. What teacher has not had the unhappy experience of planning what seemed to her a fine unit only to have it fall flat when presented to a class? Are we honest enough with ourselves to admit that often our ideas are not accepted with enthusiasm? They are followed politely, perhaps, if we are fortunate, but with no real sense of wanting to tackle a problem of importance.

Planning together, working together, and evaluating the experience together increases the pride in accomplishment because of the feeling of sharing; it takes the sting out of failure since the finger is never pointed at any one person, but the emphasis is always on the potential improvement of the group.

PLANNED SOCIALIZATION

Adolescents, especially, need many experiences that help them feel secure in the newly discovered social world that has become so important to them. As a follow-up to the list of expectations of the ninth grade class described in Chapter 4, the teacher asked each to list the five needs which seemed the most urgent to him. Overwhelmingly the choice was for:

1. How to act in a group
2. How to develop good manners for parties and other occasions
3. How to start a conversation

4. How to make friends
5. How to get over nervousness when speaking

The aggressive, the painfully shy, the withdrawing, the "apple-polisher"—all the kinds of children one finds in any class—feel the need for the skills that help them to get along with others.

There are usually many volunteers for the social committee. The teacher may wish to help organize the first one, unless there seems to be a very good reason for not doing so. After she talks it over with the whole class and discusses the qualification of a good social committee, there will usually be a compromise, and the first committee will be composed of members who have a real social sensitivity. Time must be provided for meetings. The class will often have very elaborate ideas for parties. It is best for the teacher to guide these planning sessions rather carefully so that manageable plans can be made and carried out.

Very simple and enjoyable free periods can be planned for the classroom. It is good experience for the pupils to find games that will fit the situation and to be responsible for the kinds of refreshments that will not only be easy to serve in the room but also be appropriate to the time of day. Students are delighted, and often amazed, when their teacher joins in the games just as whole-heartedly as they do. Seeing the teacher take the consequence in a game of Truth or Consequences helps immeasurably in breaking down the barriers of age and status that are so often present in teacher-pupil relationships. Laughing, playing games, and eating together—"togetherness"—is the secret of success. A kindly feeling when the refreshments turn out to be too difficult to eat, as in the case of some homemade taffy apples, helps the social committee to avoid similar mistakes the next time instead of suffering the stigma of failure. Papers on "What was good" and "What could have been better" are summarized and discussed and used as a guide for the next committee planning session.

DISCUSSION OF PERIODICALS

One way to go into group planning easily is to use periodicals. Since the core class is often a combination or replacement of English and social studies courses, one of the *Scholastic* magazines [4] lends itself admirably to class use. If possible the teacher might present several periodicals at the beginning of the year and let the class make a choice of the one it wishes to use. Suppose that the class has chosen *Scholastic*. The teacher, after the students have made a preliminary examination of the magazine, might suggest

[4] Scholastic Magazines, Inc., 50 West 44th Street, New York, New York.

that they divide into groups and make suggestions for methods of discussing the articles.

Inexperienced groups will usually suggest individual reports. As working together becomes more advanced, other possibilities are explored, such as discussion in small groups so that more can take part and feel less self-consciousness in making reports, with a follow-up report to the class on what was interesting and what methods proved successful. Each group may take a section for reports or panel discussions for the class. Sometimes one important article is discussed by the full class, and the others by groups. Sometimes a quiz program is in order. The students will find many ideas occurring to them and may apply innumerable variations of these plans. Here again is an opportunity for the teacher to establish friendly relations with her class. She may join a group and give a report as though she were one of the students, or she may sit in on the group discussion. A fine feeling of friendly sharing of problems resulted in one class when the teacher forgot to prepare her *Scholastic* report!

As pupils gain confidence in their teacher and her sincerity in accepting their ideas, they will become more creative in their suggestions for planning. If a sensible group-action evaluation takes place in the planning, the good judgment of the group usually prevails, and seldom do impossible plans pass the class scrutiny. The teacher, however, always takes an active part in all of the planning process, particularly until students gain some skill in working together.

CHAPTER 6

Techniques
of Evaluation

I n a classroom where all take part in the planning, it follows
logically that all must take part in the evaluation. Thus the
term "evaluation" necessarily broadens in scope immeasurably and
is no longer a matter of a teacher-given, factual-answer test at the
end of a unit or semester. Evaluation, then, is an integral part of
the teacher-pupil planning process, which becomes a three-part,
continuous, and integrated activity of planning-working-evaluating.
Evaluation seems to us to be the continuous questioning in many
different ways of the other two parts of the process:

1. Where are we going?
2. How are we doing?
3. How can we do better?

Evaluation begins when planning begins. To use an example:

A ninth grade class wished to make a more detailed study of
some of the broad social problems of which they had become aware.
They decided to divide into groups to be sure that all students
would be working on a topic about which they felt real concern.
(At this point the teacher always has the responsibility of pointing
out the importance of choosing a worthwhile problem, and evaluation begins). The class set up a list of criteria for choosing a problem. (Since the purpose of referring to a set of criteria for choosing
problems is different from that described in Chapter 3, we repeat
an example.) Everyone agreed upon the importance of these criteria, which were brush-penned on a large sheet of paper and
posted for all to see.

Criteria for Selecting a Problem

A problem must:
1. Be really useful to us

2. Apply to all of us
3. Afford everybody an opportunity to work on it
4. Have plenty of materials available
5. Be interesting to all of us
6. Help develop basic skills
7. Be worth spending our time on

Such a set of criteria helps a group of pupils to clarify their purpose. It gives them a vocabulary with which to voice their objections or defend their choices. It gives them security that they are planning and choosing a problem that is really worthwhile. In other words, it helps them to evaluate.

This process is not simple. Evaluation as an end product is much more simple. People do not always find it easy to look at what they are doing objectively and try to improve. Once the basic concept of evaluation as an ongoing process is accepted by the teacher and eventually by the students, many techniques and devices may be discovered by which group and individual procedures can be improved. This concept of evaluation gives both a sense of completeness to the planning processes and a sense of continuing worth; for we evaluate not in terms of what is over and done with and about which we can no longer do anything, but in terms of how all experiences can be applied to future activities to make them better. Evaluation photographs, as it were, what we are doing for critical scrutiny in order to point toward better ways of working. Evaluation then becomes a learning experience.

In effective group processes people grow in an intangible way. Such growth is usually the most difficult to measure, but often represents the most important progress. Students have to be helped to recognize and measure this kind of growth. Many still think of evaluation as getting one hundred on a test, for all of us find it difficult to discard the long-accepted standards. Soon, however, they will begin to recognize the value of other kinds of progress. They will put value, for example, in the increase in self-confidence that results from making a business phone call; on the broadening of outlook that comes from reading a magazine article dealing with a controversial problem; on arranging and participating in an interview with someone of another race or country. Does not growth in self-confidence, in reading and thinking skills, in attitudes toward those different from ourselves, have a much more far-reaching effect than the grade of one hundred on a test? We do not discredit or minimize the value of a test when it fits the immediate need, but we wish that it were only one kind of evaluating technique rather than an end in itself.

As an example of one student's recognition of the value of

growth in human relationships, we point to Robert. He appeared to be a self-centered, antisocial boy. He found great difficulty in adjusting to group work, exemplified by frequent disagreements and withdrawals. Both Robert and the teacher felt that progress of lasting worth had been made when he wrote: "When I first came into this class and anyone would ask me to borrow a pencil, I would say, 'Get your own. Don't always ask to use mine.' Today Ed asked to use my eraser, and I gave it to him and felt good about it." The very recognition of improvement showed growth on Robert's part. His relationships with his fellow classmates had become more satisfying both to him and to them.

The examples of various kinds of evaluation to follow will include constant attempt to measure the intangibles. Grading in the accepted term becomes minimized; recognizing all kinds of progress and facilitating future activities becomes the objective of evaluation.

TYPES OF ORAL EVALUATION

Daily evaluation. Some teachers like to reserve a small part of each day's class time for evaluation. This can be very worthwhile if it does not become repetitious. Perhaps at the beginning of the period the teacher or student chairman might ask questions of this nature:

"How are we getting along in our work?"

"Are any groups having any special difficulties?"

"What are our plans for today?"

"What are we trying to accomplish today?"

This is essentially an evaluation of what is going on and how the work is progressing. It also lays out the procedure for ensuing work.

Perhaps at the end of the class period the teacher or student chairman might pose questions such as these:

"How did we get along today?"

"Does anyone have any special problems?"

"Are we accomplishing as much as we had hoped to accomplish?"

"What plans have we made for tomorrow?"

The type of questions vary with the situation, of course. A daily checkup of this kind is good for both teacher and pupils. It gives the teacher a chance to catch up on what is going on and it helps to organize the work of the class. Such simple techniques can help to pull a group together and keep the work focused on the purposes and results.

Class discussion. In this type of evaluation the entire class and the teacher can take an active part. Here the questions and points to be considered can be prepared in advance by the teacher, a student, a group of students working with the teacher, or any suitable combination of these persons. The questions would obviously be based on the purposes previously set up for the activity to be evaluated. A competent student can lead the discussion or it can be divided into several parts so that more students can have experience as discussion leaders. If students have not attained sufficient skill to lead a discussion, however, the teacher should serve as the leader.

While a general discussion does not usually give each person an opportunity to express himself on every point under consideration, it does allow the thinking of the entire group to come forth. Ideas expressed by one lead to further ideas on the part of others.

This technique works well when a class has progressed together to a point where a good discussion can be held. Sometimes at the beginning of the year it is difficult to hold a satisfactory class discussion because pupils have not gained the necessary listening and reaction skills. After they have advanced in these skills the general class discussion is an effective evaluative technique.

Panel evalutaion. To vary evaluation sessions a sampling of group feeling can be made by asking four or five pupils to serve on a panel to discuss an activity just concluded. The members of the panel can plan their presentation in advance, going over the various points together and perhaps asking other members of the class for their opinions. A student chairman can handle this session and, following the panel discussion, the entire class can participate. In this way the various aspects of the evaluation can be pinpointed and then discussed by the entire group. This method also provides valuable experience for those serving on the panel and good listening practice for the rest of the group.

Small groups reporting to total groups. Another evaluation technique that involves everyone is that of having the groups that worked on a project discuss the evaluation questions in their groups for a given amount of time. They then report their conclusions to the total group. This process can be handled easily by a student discussion leader. He has only to call on the chairmen or recorders of the various groups for their reports. Time can be allotted for total group discussion following the reports. A written record of the reports might be made in order to have a permanent record and also to give experience to pupils in compiling and organizing such data. Repetition in the oral reports can be avoided by asking the pupils to report only on ideas not previously mentioned, or on some new aspect of an idea.

Using the tape recorder for evaluations. Nothing is quite so fascinating to young people as making a recording of their own voices. They really enjoy hearing themselves when the tape is played back, and, in addition, they learn some valuable things about their voices and speech habits.

Recording an evaluation discussion can present some problems because it takes a good deal of time to record the conversation and then to play it back. However, the discussion can be limited in time, highlighting only major points. This in itself is good experience. When the tape is played back, the class can readily see just where they have failed to do a good job on the evaluation. The teacher can identify irrelevant statements, the person who talks too much, the giggler, the mumbler, all in the spirit of friendly yet meaningful criticism.

Evaluating the study group. From time to time it is a good plan for the small study groups to evaluate themselves and their work. The teacher might suggest that they spend fifteen minutes of their study time one or two days a week asking themselves whether their work is progressing satisfactorily toward their purposes. They can discuss what they are doing and how, and suggest improvements, if necessary. This technique serves to unite group efforts and to organize study procedures. The results of these evaluations might be reported very briefly to the total group by the chairmen of the small groups. This kind of sharing of ideas can be of benefit to everyone.

Spot-observer evaluation. Two or three students volunteer or are appointed to be spot observers for the day. They make their observations on the basis of which practices they think are good and which they think could be better.

Five minutes before the end of the class day, the observers report their findings. Objectivity is encouraged. This type of observing helps students to look constructively at what is going on about them.

Evaluation of class discussion. During a class discussion the teacher might interrupt, after taking careful note of certain factors, to say: "I have been watching you closely during this discussion, and I seem to see that about twenty people are listening attentively. This is about sixty-six percent of our class. Fifteen are participating in the discussion, but only about five are carrying the burden of it. Am I wrong, or is my observation correct?" This may be followed by some suggestions to improve the discussion. It is invariably followed by better attention and participation. After the teacher makes this type of observation a few times, students will often pick up the idea and voluntarily report their own observations.

A similar device is to keep and later copy on the board a little chart, in which the dots represent the number of students:

	Listening	Discussing
	. . . .	. . .
10:00	. . . .	
10:05	. . . .	. .
	. . . .	. . . .
10:10	. . . .	. . . .

This type of visual organization often appeals to some who otherwise participate little in discussions, and they will voluntarily keep charts. It also helps to lead the class into an analysis of what constitutes a good discussion, what each person's role is in a discussion, and what factors lead to a lack of interest or participation.

TYPES OF WRITTEN EVALUATION

Written evaluations can be as varied as oral evaluations. Their chief value lies in the fact that the students have an opportunity to record their opinions in a permanent form. The evaluation can be made out by the teacher, the students, or a combination of both. Writing out one's thoughts gives practice not only in organizing and clarifying thinking, but also in penmanship, spelling, correct English usage, punctuation, and sentence structure. Included at the end of this chapter are several types of evaluations that have been used in classrooms.

Quizzes and tests. Quizzes and tests are the time-honored form of evaluation. They can be used effectively in many situations. They are most valuable when they serve the purpose of allowing the student to show what he has learned. Again, teachers or pupils or both can compose tests. Students are likely to make the questions far too difficult for their peers until they have had considerable experience. It is wise, therefore, for the teacher to keep a watchful eye on the proceedings.

Self-evaluation. Evaluating oneself is a task that few of us like and even fewer actually do. Time, integrity, and skill are necessary. Thus pupils find self-evaluation difficult, sometimes unpleasant; but teachers find this process extremely valuable in helping pupils to face problems and to work and think independently at the same time they are learning how to work with others. Then, too, as long as most school systems require that letter grades be given as an evaluative measure of a student's work, the technique of having students evaluate themselves is a great help to the teacher. When working with pupils democratically, asking that each student contribute what he can as well as he can, it is almost impossible to be autocratic in administering grades without working against the cooperative spirit the teacher has tried to establish.

While self-evaluation plays a part in practically all the samples at the end of this chapter, a different type is illustrated in Sample I. The form was compiled from the class goals by groups and the teacher. At the end of each marking period the teacher and pupils usually agreed on the grades earned, but when there was a marked difference a conference helped with clarification. The teacher obviously must be willing to listen and to be as flexible as necessary. If she has developed a good relationship with her students, she should experience little difficulty. Most rewarding is the absence of hard feelings that so often accompany giving grades.

The weekly log. The weekly log is another effective evaluation device. When it is first used the reaction is often one of defensiveness or resentment. Pupils are not sure whether or not they may safely say what they think. After the first summary, however, made by the teacher and kept entirely impersonal without pointing the finger at any one person, they no longer take criticisms personally; they begin to try to improve situations that they often did not fully recognize as being detrimental to good group accomplishment.

On Monday morning the pupils hand in to the teacher the evaluation of the previous week's work. Everyone has in his notebook a copy of the class goals, of the log questions, and a schedule of the week (see Sample J).

The teacher summarizes the logs for discussion within the next day or two. This is a time-consuming task, but it reaps such rewards that it is worth the effort. Immediate attention to the summary is important so that immediate improvement can take place. From the summary the teacher discusses each question, omitting no comment, however slight. Where matters of petty criticism or deep basic hostilities are involved, the anonymity of the discussion makes each person tend to be objective about his own behavior. After reading the summary the teacher will ask for discussion. Out of this discussion will often come valuable suggestions for improved activities and methods of working together. Group meetings will be held, and groups will discuss the problems peculiar to them. Usually, immediate improvement will follow such statements as:

"One person in our group refuses to help us, but I think he is a little better this week than last."

"There is a little clique in our class that tries to run everything. I think we should all be friendly with everybody."

"Two girls in our group talk and giggle about their boyfriends instead of getting down to work."

"Some of the people in our group talk to the people in Group III."

"Our chairman goes walking around the room instead of helping us get started on our project."

"I think the recorders should make better notes."

"Two people in our group chew gum all the time."

Discussing such problems openly and impersonally can have a therapeutic effect on both the individual and the group. If much of the work of the class is done in small groups, it is a responsibility of the teacher to teach students how to work together. No problem is too trivial for some attention. Discussing problems of human relationships has a wholesome effect on students. They recognize that problems are myriad and that no one is without them. They are comforted by the fact that often problems are general and not unique, and they are encouraged when either group or individual progress is noted.

The log is so designed that not all comments will be derogatory. Everyone feels pride when such statements as these appear:

. "I think our class chairman did a very fine job this week."

"The planning committee is improving. The schedule looked nice on the board, and the time was planned better."

"I liked the reports on the tape recorder. I think Group IV showed a lot of originality in presenting their project."

"The social committee planned a snack and game that were fun this week."

"The bulletin boards looked much better."

"The boys in our class are becoming more polite. One boy stood aside and let me go out the door first."

The teacher, too, comes in for her share of the criticism. Some say: "The teacher is doing fine and couldn't do better." Pleasant, though not very constructive! Often there will be a statement like "The teacher should put her foot down more often and make us do what she says." This in contrast to "Our teacher should be more democratic and let us run things ourselves more. I think we would take more responsibility if she would give us a chance."

These statements show widely varying reactions to the same situations and give the teacher an opportunity to help students think through the problems of democratic government and the necessity for individual and group readiness. After the teacher shows good faith, reading and discussing frankly all criticisms, the students become more constructive and show better results.

There is a certain value in using the same log questions for several weeks. A pattern of thinking is then established, and during the week pupils think in terms of this evaluation. The example given can be simplified or varied. Another set of questions, such as the ones that follow, might be summarized a bit more easily:

What did we accomplish this week?

What did we fail to accomplish this week?

What suggestions do I have for class improvements?

What is my idea of the role of the teacher in our class?

In addition to the class use of the log material, the teacher finds it a rich source of suggestions for helping individuals and establishing close relationships with them. A little extra time for an aside like: "Are you feeling more at home in your group, Ray?" or "Do you think the girls in your group are doing better this week, Tom?" gives each student the feeling that the teacher is sincerely interested in him and that something is being done about his problems as well as just his gripes.

The log material is potent with opportunities of all kinds in the dynamics of the class. To us it seems almost an imperative kind of evaluation technique in classes of the kind described in this book.

Group evaluation. Group evaluation is mandatory when pupils are working together in small groups. The planning for evaluating should begin almost as soon as the work begins. An example of combining self- and group evaluation was given in Chapter 5 as a part of the Fields of Work Project. Samples K and L suggest additional variations. The entire class may also set up the criteria for rating the presentation of each group as in Samples K, L, and M.

COMBINING ORAL AND WRITTEN EVALUATION

Committee evaluation. The following plan has been used very effectively: A committee from the class evaluated everyone's contribution to a project. A very important factor is the choice of the committee, for each member should have certain qualifications. First, he must wish to work on the committee and be willing to put in the extra time necessary; second, he must have the trust and good faith of the class so that his judgment will be accepted.

More than half the class volunteered to work on the committee in Sample N. The teacher then had the class vote on those whom they considered to have the skills to judge fairly, without bias. Because the goals and requirements of the project were a part of the evaluation, the typed sheet that every pupil had is reproduced here in Sample N.

The semester evaluation. After a semester or a year of working together, teachers and pupils recognize the need for an overall look at their experience. Perhaps these papers should be unsigned, to insure free replies, although few pupils who have worked in such an atmosphere expect punitive measures. There are usually several areas that the teacher wishes evaluated; thus the questions must be pertinent to the period and designed to give pupils opportunity for recall and for unsolicited comments.

Questions designed for a tenth grade block in English and world history covered many aspects of the class activities:

I. Do you feel that the class was valuable to you from the standpoint of:
   A. Helping you to get along with others?
   B. Helping you to think for yourself?
II. Do you prefer a combined class meeting for two hours or single classes meeting for one hour only? Please tell why.
III. Were there special things about this class that you:
   A. Liked?
   B. Disliked?
IV. Do you feel that you learned English and world history?
V. Did you profit from having your own class library?
VI. In what ways might our class have been improved?
VII. Have the things we learned helped you in your work this year?

Responses to such questions, negative or constructive, point the way to new challenges for the teacher. Such comments as the following are gratifying: "It helped me to get better acquainted with other students. I think the better you know a person and understand him, the better you can get along with him." But the following kinds of comments force a teacher to reexamine her own value: "I don't feel that as much is accomplished in this type of class" or "The class could have been improved by more grammar," "more history," or "better manners from students." And if we ask our students to reexamine, must we not do it also?

Pupil-teacher planning is a creative way of teaching. Evaluation is a part of the process, and the teacher's and the pupils' skill in evaluating grows as their ability to plan together grows. Teachers who are earnestly working to plan with their pupils will find many effective ways of evaluating in addition to those given here. We hope these examples will tend to broaden the field of evaluation beyond the "feeding-back-of-knowledge" process so well known to all of us.

Sample G

SUMMARY AND EVALUATION OF

SOCIAL PROBLEMS PROJECT

(Hand in Tuesday, November 21)

Name_____ Group_____ Problem _____

1. I contributed the following work and materials to our project:

2. I interviewed the following people for information:

3. I read the following books and articles: (Be specific.)

4. Values of the project to me in terms of what I learned and the time consumed (approximately ten hours of class time plus my outside work):

5. My group rated my contribution_____.

Signed _____ , Chairman
_____ , Recorder

Sample H

PUPIL'S PROGRESS REPORT

Name _____ Date _____

Direction to students: After you have completed an activity, you may use this sheet to help you decide just how worthwhile this work was to you.

1. Type of activity

2. Time spent: Number of days_____ Average amount each day_____

3. Are you satisfied with the things you accomplished during the time spent on this activity? Yes_____ No_____
   Explain:

4. Did you learn any new ways of doing things while working on this activity? Yes_____ No_____ If so, what?

5. Did you change your mind about anything while working on this subject? Yes_____ No_____ If so, what?

6. While working on this activity have you become interested in anything that you would like to know more about or to continue working at in your spare time? Yes_____ No_____ If so, what?

Sample I

SELF EVALUATION

	First Marking Period		Second Marking Period		Third Marking Period	
	S	T	S	T	S	T*
I. Accepting responsibility						
A. Getting work done on time						
B. Paying class dues						
C. Bringing library books						
D. Keeping files up to date						
II. Self-control						
A. Committee meetings						
B. Class discussions and meetings						
C. When teacher is gone						
III. Attitudes						
A. Toward other students						
B. Toward school politics						
C. Toward work						
D. Toward teacher						
E. Toward responsibilities						
IV. Oral and written English						
A. Spelling						
B. Grammar						
C. Speaking						
D. Punctuation						
E. Sentences						
F. Paragraphing						
V. Neatness of paper						
A. Writing						
B. Form						
C. Carelessness						
D. Condition of paper						
VI. Using time wisely						
A. Free time						
B. Free reading						
C. Committee time						
D. Concentration						
VII. Contributing to class meetings and discussions						
A. Participation						
B. Voting						
C. Being Prepared						
D. Paying attention						
VIII. Knowledge gained						
A. Facts						
B. Understanding						
C. New ideas and opinions						

*S = student.　　T = teacher.

Sample J

WEEKLY LOG

Log No. _____ Name _____

Date _____ Group No. _____

I. The class
   A. What were our best accomplishments this week?
   B. What could we do better?

II. My group
   A. How did I improve, especially in terms of our goals?
   B. What blocks the work of our group?

III. Myself
   A. How did I improve, especially in terms of our goals?
   B. What plans do I have for further improvements?

IV. The teacher
   A. What can the teacher do to be more helpful to us?
   B. What do I wish we could do differently?

Sample K

EVALUATION OF PROJECTS
SOCIAL LIVING

I. Oral evaluation of each group presentation by the class
   A. Did everyone participate in the discussion?
   B. How much work seemed to go into the project?
   C. Was it interestingly presented?
   D. Did it help us with our problems?

II. Evaluation of the individual by himself and his group

Tear off. Recorder hand in all evaluations.

Name _____ Group number ____

A. Who contributed most to our project?_____
_____

B. How well did our group cooperate? _____
_____

C. What did I gain from this project? _____
_____

D. Grade given me by my group _____ Citizenship_____

E. Any additional comments:

(Note: This evaluation was planned by Group III and Miss Barrett.)

Sample L

GROUP EVALUATION OF GOVERNMENT UNIT

Names _____ Grade _____ Citizenship ___

_____ _____ _____

_____ _____ _____

_____ _____ _____

_____ _____ _____

The group is to determine the quality of work which each person did. Consider neatness and completeness of outline as well as work in the group.

_____ _____ _____

A is a perfect grade in every sense.
B indicates very good work
C is average, acceptable but not outstanding.
D is poor.
E indicates no contribution and an incomplete outline.

A 1 citizen is one who is the best and most reliable, willing to take responsibility, willing to lead and follow, always cheerful, pleasant, dependable, considerate, working for the good of the group rather than just self-interest.

Citizenship ratings of 2,3,4,5 are based on 1 in lesser degrees.

This rating process will be difficult. No one should consider it a personal matter, but rather a matter of group responsibility. The group may use its own method of deciding on the grades, but talking over what each person has done will help everyone in the future.

The above grades were fairly agreed upon by the whole group, and we certify them to be correct.

Signed _____ , Chairman
Group No. _____ _____ , Recorder

In addition, the class rates each group upon its presentation, after setting up a list of criteria (see Samples K and M).

Sample M

CLASS EVALUATION OF GROUP REPORTS

(Criteria for class evaluation of each group presentation were
planned by the whole class in a general discussion during the preparation of the unit)

I. Presentation of reports
   A. Grammar
   B. Voice
   C. Choice of words
   D. Posture and poise
   E. Skill in using notes
   F. Audience reaction indicating degree of interest

II. Organization of project
   A. Planning
   B. Original ways of arousing interest
   C. Total group participation
   D. Value of test

Sample N

SOCIAL PROBLEMS PROJECT

Name _____

I. Goals
   In working on this project, our class hopes to achieve some
   success in the following goals:
   A. Learning about the topics: Marriage, Divorce, Juvenile
      Delinquency
   B. Learning to plan together
   C. Learning to work together
   D. Learning to participate in group planning and work
   E. Learning to work independently
   F. Learning to find and use material
   G. Learning to use time wisely
   H. Sharing information
   I. Finding interesting and effective ways of presenting
      material
   J. Improving manners

    K. Improving communications skills
      1. Speaking
        Becoming more conscious of grammar errors
      2. Listening
        In groups during planning
        To reports, for the purpose of learning
      3. Writing
      4. Reading
        Especially learning to read material on an unfamiliar
        subject

  II. Minimum requirements
    A. Read the chapters in the text
    B. Read two additional references
    C. Give one oral report
    D. Make one written report

 III. Optional
    Making displays; interviewing; extra reports; extra writing;
    extra reading

 IV. Bibliography
    Reference   Article or chapter   Comment

CHAPTER 7

Human Relations

esearch has indicated to educators that real learning is best accomplished in a pleasant, relaxed atmosphere. The learner must be free from frustrations and fear in order to absorb and understand the materials with which he is dealing. Whether he is studying calculus, Latin, the social sciences, baking a cake or building a bookcase, he cannot do his best work and receive the maximum benefits from it if the situation is tense and forbidding.

Realizing this, a modern teacher will make a sincere effort to recognize individual differences and to improve human relations in her classroom. To ignore the emotional problems existing in any given group and to place major emphasis on subject matter alone does not eliminate the problems. Many times this course of action tends to intensify emotions and to release aggressions that result in undisciplined behavior, confusion, hostility toward school, unhappiness and failure.

A core-type class, with its extended time allotment, gives increased opportunity for the teacher to study the personal problems of her students and to stimulate the group processes that help solve these problems. Since one of the goals of the core-type class is to help pupils get along better together, the teacher has a direct responsibility in this area. Every classroom has its quota of many types of personalities: the introverts and extroverts, the isolates, the rejects, the insecure, the slow and the brilliant, the jealous, and the prejudiced. The teacher who does not ignore the existence of these problems must find ways of dealing with them.

Despite the uniqueness of each individual, every teacher has learned to recognize certain types of boys and girls who follow given patterns of behavior. The following anecdotes are accounts of real people and actual happenings relating to fairly common problems in human relations. They are included here to illustrate how pupil-teacher planning can help to solve such problems.

PUPILS WHO LACK SELF-CONFIDENCE

Maryann was a shy, retiring, conscientious girl. She did beautiful written work, was always perfectly prepared and attentive, raised her hand for the "right answers," and smiled shyly at the teacher occasionally. She had no conversation with her fellow students, and she flushed in an embarrassed way whenever she had any unexpected contact with them. She had a girlfriend or two in the class. She was always the model student. Maryann was, in fact, the ideal student for a class in which the flow of learning was from teacher to pupil and the requirements were limited to behaving decorously and completing one's lessons.

The teacher soon recognized Maryann's problem of extreme shyness as a serious one in a class where much of the work was to be done eventually in small groups. She became interested in finding ways to help Maryann to become more at ease with her peers. Written papers, which seemed a release for the girl, indicated home problems. She wrote: "When I was little, my father drank and I was always ashamed to take anyone to my home for fear of what he would do. Now I am so shy that I do not go out much, and I have no boyfriends." A conference with Maryann's mother at PTA added to the teacher's understanding of Maryann's shyness. The mother recognized the problem, saying that the father often teased the girl, who had no skills of repartee and thus suffered from such teasing.

Students are often quick to recognize academic worth. In her first group experience, although Maryann sat back shyly and did not participate in the conversation of the group, she was elected recorder. The teacher made it a point to be near her often to give her security, and helped her with the details of recording so that she would not lose the feeling of academic success. She had to give some simple reports for her group to the class, and although she always flushed with embarrassment, she habitually did what was expected of her. Her circle of girlfriends widened, and she had obvious respect in the class because of her sense of responsibility. Class parties drew her into a different kind of group participation, and she began participating more normally in such activities.

A later conference with her mother at PTA gave this insight: "I can't tell you how happy I am at the change that has taken place in Maryann. She now takes her own part when her father teases her. She is happier at home and at school. The other day she said to me, 'Mother, what do you think happened today at school? I spoke to a BOY!' "

Important to an adolescent? Maryann would always achieve academic success. What of her need for social success? Does not the school have a very real responsibility toward young people who have acute problems of social adjustment? Maryann's extreme withdrawing tendencies might have led to serious emotional problems in later years. The freedom to try her wings without pressure or fear of punishment undoubtedly set a new and more normal pattern of behavior for her whole life.

Walt presents a different kind of situation. In addition to many personality problems resulting from a meager experiential background, a strictly disciplined and religiously prejudiced home, and a small physical stature, Walt had a very serious speech defect. He refused to talk at all in class, always hiding behind someone in any discussion, although he would talk to the teacher. Like Maryann, he was able to get some degree of security from her. Walt informed the teacher early in the first week that he could not write, that he could never think of anything to say, and that he couldn't spell. She soon discovered that he spelled phonetically, as he spoke!

Near the beginning of the year, Walt volunteered to be responsible to see that tables and chairs were in order at the end of the morning. The teacher commended him on his attention to detail in this matter, and he doubled his efforts to keep the room neat. Meantime he contributed little to his group and always tried to sit somewhat withdrawn.

When permanent committees were organized, Walt became a member of the room committee and was elected chairman by the less ambitious members. His first public appearance as a speaker in the class came during a business meeting, when he made a report for his committee. It was something in the nature of a scolding, as well as a request for better cooperation. The next week Walt commended the class for cooperation in this matter. His group work began to improve, and he made some definite contributions to a project. His feeling of status improved his academic achievement, and he amazed himself by writing a two-page paper on space travel! Socially, he was becoming more skilled and did not need all his security from the teacher. One day he surprised everyone by volunteering to give the summary of an oral evaluation of the week's work for his group, and it was a very fine ten-minute discussion.

It must be remembered that the class and the groups are growing as well as the individuals, and the "we" feeling in the group helps greatly in the solution of the problems of individuals. Frank discussion of problems brings out the fact that we all have them, and that while some will always be there, few are insurmountable when we learn to live with other people. Later successes on Walt's part were recognized and commended by the class. The most mature and tactful girl in the class was one day moved to comment on Walt's former habit of hiding behind someone to avoid talking and on the progress he had made. Walt smiled appreciatively, and a good feeling of sharing his success was a result. The ability to discuss progress is one of the marks of the emotional and social maturity achieved in a class of this kind.

LOW ACADEMIC ACHIEVEMENT

The teacher must be alert to the plans of all groups to avoid the possibility of too much pressure on any pupil of low academic ability. Helen entered ninth grade from a small county school. She was pathetically eager to please the teacher and made friendly advances toward her classmates. Her IQ was in the 80's and she was a year or two older than others in the class.

Helen had learned the ways to please teachers. She tidied up the room often and brought pictures from home. Fortunately, she was in a group with a very tactful leader. The group early developed a feeling of group pride, and Helen was given help in the presentation of simple news reports on the day her group was responsible. She made herself very useful when the group made a scrapbook, and she was able to share in the feeling of success of the project. As the class learned more about individual differences and the importance of every person's contribution, Helen was accepted and treated with the same liking and respect as the more academically gifted.

At the end of the year Helen wrote this poignant commentary: "This is the best class I have ever been in. When I started to school the kids liked me up to the third grade. From the third through the eighth grade the kids didn't like me. In this class everybody is nice. The kids don't laugh at me or make fun of me."

Academic pressure would undoubtedly have resulted in failure and unhappiness for this girl. Group work gave her an opportunity for success to the limits of her ability, and the satisfaction of knowing she had made a valued contribution to her class.

HIGH ACADEMIC ACHIEVEMENT

One of the problems of teaching is the difficulty of challenging sufficiently the real student, the brilliant mind that grasps so readily what the normal and below normal must work to achieve. A class in which teacher-pupil planning and group work predominate seems to take care of this lag. True, at the beginning of pupil participation in the planning, the student who is working for a straight A record often feels frustration and insecurity when he sees that he is not always having the opportunity of succeeding in the accepted pattern. The teacher must be alert to such worries and help the brighter student to begin to see his way clear to a service role in the class as well as an academic success role. Many times, more often than not in fact, these students are leaders and can expend much of their energy and ability in the leadership role.

Such a student was Jeanne. She had, in addition to her academic ability, a personality of unusual charm, a real liking for people, and an experiential and family educational background above the average. With all of these advantages she was modest and even reticent about assuming a leadership role. Unconsciously, she seemed to recognize her mental superiority and attempted to conform to a more nearly average pattern. Her personal attractiveness and clever ideas about dress and grooming soon made her the object of imitation by most of the girls in the class. She was always friendly and chatty and entered into all activities of the class so wholeheartedly that even the nonacademic boys trusted her sincerity.

Now, what could challenge Jeanne to a real sense of achievement in our class? As a member of the bulletin board committee she kept the group working harmoniously and productively. She helped plan parties, became Student Council representative, led discussions when asked, and participated willingly in all class activities. It was in the field of human relations, however, that Jeanne received her greatest challenge and achieved her greatest personal satisfaction. She was invariably elected a group leader, and her groups always worked well together. In meetings of group leaders and in personal contacts with Jeanne, the teacher always stressed that a leader could accept and get along with group members better if he would try to understand their behavior. Many student leaders are too immature or too limited in other ways to follow such suggestions very seriously, but to Jeanne they were challenging. She read many books and pamphlets on human relations. She was extremely interested in learning of the basic needs of all human beings as interpreted in our personal and social problems discussions. As her understanding grew, she became more tactful and more self-assured.

One day each group chairman was giving an informal summary of how well the group worked together on a certain project. Jeanne represented a group of six students, none of whom was outstanding academically. Indeed, as she made her report, she sat next to small undernourished Bud—low IQ, reading level, third grade. In summary, Jeanne said with the utmost sincerity and in a voice which was obviously moved: "This is the finest group I have ever worked with. Everybody cooperated, and—well—we've just had a wonderful time together." Her statement was followed by a hush. I think we all shared the conviction that something wonderful had happened in our class—to all of us.

The opportunity to develop her latent skills with people would scarcely have come to Jeanne in a class where students had little freedom of action. She had already established habits of success in academic achievement. Many times a superior student is isolated from his fellows by his very superiority, when it should be a means to a much higher goal of service and leadership in human relations.

At the end of her year's experience Jeanne wrote as follows: "I feel that my year in G. E. has been one of my most satisfying experiences thus far in my school life. When I first came into this class I thought to myself, 'What a boring time I'll have with the same group of boys and girls and to top that off the same teacher for three straight hours.' Was I surprised! I immediately felt right at home (usually I don't for awhile) and took a liking to my friendly teacher. This class has been like one big happy family to me, and I've actually looked forward to coming to school in the mornings this past year. This class has done more to give me self-confidence than any one thing I know. I very highly recommend it to incoming 9B's."

THE REJECTED CHILD

Larry was a model of cleanliness and good grooming. He was physically fit, though a bit on the heavy side. His intelligence, however, was far below normal and every day brought new frustrations in the form of school work. He was so overwrought that he broke into tears when the teacher offered to help him. If she came near him as he was writing something, his hand shook so that he could hardly hold the pencil on the paper. To add to his misery, he was completely rejected by the other pupils.

Larry's teacher encouraged him to enter into activities in the class, creating a place for him where none existed. She demanded very little of him in the way of academic achievement because she knew there could be very little. She gave him many odd jobs to do to keep him busy and made sure that the other pupils treated him with consideration. They saw that he was not to bear the brunt of her wrath because of his inabilities but rather that she was offering him help, encouragement, and friendship. Their attitudes changed somewhat. They picked up her cues and found things that Larry could do in working groups. In fact, the actions of the other pupils became almost protective toward the unfortunate Larry. One day a student chairman selected him to report on an event concerning the national elections and one of the other boys said, "Larry doesn't like to read the newspapers. Why can't he call on us for our reports?"

That was a wonderful solution to an unhappy situation and the pupils themselves came forth with it. Larry's existence in that classroom gradually became more enjoyable. The attitude of his teacher was reflected in the other pupils, and while he was not really accepted as "one of the gang" in social circles, he was not ridiculed or rejected completely. Pupil-teacher planning helped Larry to find a place for himself and it helped to build better appreciations and attitudes in the other pupils.

THE AGGRESSIVE CHILD

Betty was a lovely girl to look at. She had taffy-colored hair that turned up pertly at the ends, matching the tilt of her sharp little nose. In Betty's case beauty was truly only skin deep. She began the semester docilely enough, but as time wore on and she became more confident of herself, her true colors came to the fore.

Once the teacher stopped to watch her as she was working on a bulletin board display and gently criticized a part of the work. Betty's temper flared. She sighed audibly and said, "Well, we can't all be perfect."

Her teacher was taken aback for the moment but gave no outward sign. She merely said, "No, you're right, I guess we can't," and walked away. This left Betty rather deflated and so of course she became defensive. She assumed a bored, scornful air and at the slightest provocation made impudent remarks directed at her teacher. She tried to impress her friends by bragging loudly that Miss Edwards wasn't going to tell her what to do, and that she would just tell Miss Edwards exactly what she thought of her.

The situation grew worse instead of better in spite of the fact that Betty's teacher tried to ignore her insults and to improve her negative attitudes by substituting activities that she thought Betty would enjoy. However, Betty's attitudes began to influence others in the group and when she became vociferous in unreasonable objections to some project the group had undertaken, Miss Edwards decided to act more directly.

The first step she took was to assure Betty while all the class was listening that she had every right to voice her opinion and that her views should be taken into consideration as much as anyone's. Then after class she asked Betty if she would come to her office after school was over. Betty said, "Oh, I suppose so, if I have to stay after school."

That afternoon they had a long talk. Miss Edwards arrived a few minutes late deliberately. She walked into her office carrying two Cokes, gave one to Betty, and settled herself comfortably in one of the chairs—not behind the desk. They talked about things Betty was doing and what she would like to be working on, never referring to her negative attitudes and sharp tongue. Betty made the comment that the work was just "kid stuff" and she was tired of it. Miss Edwards told her that she was capable of doing more advanced work because she was a mature thinker and suggested that she find better ways of spending her time to utilize her talents.

By the time the conference ended Miss Edwards was more hopeful about the situation. She felt that Betty had enjoyed the relaxed, informal talk and had had an opportunity to express her feelings. Also, Betty had been given a challenge. Of course, Miss Edwards would watch very carefully to make sure that the work Betty chose to do offered her a real challenge.

Here the teacher made a real effort to make friends with a student. Instead of reacting sharply to the child's aggressiveness, she took it calmly and offered her sympathetic understanding as well as a solution to her problems. She was gratified when at the end of the year she found an envelope on her desk containing a note from Betty. Two statements made a year's work seem well worth the effort: "I think you're one of the fairest of all my teachers. I just wanted to tell you how much I have enjoyed being in your class this year."

PUPILS WITH SPECIAL TALENTS

Students with special talents often progress through their entire school career with their talents unrecognized by teachers. Fellow students may know that a boy is an expert on model airplanes or that a girl has remarkable dancing ability, but teachers are seldom privileged to share the secret. These students, gifted in such varied ways, may find that in the teacher's eyes they are only mediocre. Their real abilities and interests rarely fit into the classroom world of courses of study and competitive standards, and they fall behind. They are "nobodies" going through the motions of doing the required work, but waiting only for the bell to ring to release them. Then they can pursue their interests elsewhere. Then their self-esteem rises and their status among their peers improves a hundredfold. On the other hand, these especially talented students may get along most satisfactorily, complying with all the rules and achieving success academically. But how much richer classroom experiences could be if these special talents could be utilized in the learning situation for the benefit of all.

In a classroom where students have a share in the planning, we often find that special talents among students find their way into activities of the small working groups and the group as a whole. Students discover these special talents much sooner than teachers and put them to use without unnecessary concern, accepting them with due respect and admiration. Teachers who work closely with students and who make an effort to learn something about students' interests and abilities may uncover these special talents and tactfully make them known at appropriate times.

Following are some typical cases in which special talents were utilized to the advantage of all in classroom situations.

Susan, as a seventh grader, was a tiny, dark-eyed, quiet child. Had her English-social studies teacher not made an effort to help her participate in group activities she would have remained in the background. Her written work would have been acceptable, but she never would have been recognized for her special gift, which was acting. The teacher had noticed, while observing her group in the halls, that Susan was gay and laughing with her own friends. She teased the others, played practical jokes on them, spoke with animation, and was seemingly quite self-possessed. All this was in direct contrast to her behavior in the classroom, where she rarely spoke to anyone and then only in a very guarded manner.

One day when committees for a *Junior Scholastic* discussion were being organized, Susan's teacher made it a point to ask whether she would serve on a committee composed of several of her special friends. Susan agreed and the group went to work to plan a review of the article assigned to them. They decided to dramatize the report and Susan fell heir to the part of a humorous character who played a leading role. When the skit was presented, the class and the teacher were amazed to see the retiring Susan in a completely different light. Her acting was a great success and her status in the group rose immediately. The students discovered that she was not the mouselike little creature they had thought and from that time on would not let her slip back into that assumed role. Susan soon seemed to relax and lose her fear of the classroom situation. She participated much more actively in group projects and, with the resulting lessening of tension, improved greatly in her work.

Another student was, as a tenth grader, an obstreperous, conceited, brilliant, uninhibited boy called Jim. He liked nothing better than to heckle his teachers and classmates and was able to earn superior grades without much effort. When he entered tenth grade core he viewed the class as an opportunity to do very little in the way of work and to get exactly what he wanted from the others by outtalking and outmaneuvering them. He was a complete misfit from the beginning. The other students hated him thoroughly, but Jim continued to bludgeon his way through.

His teacher was immediately aware of him and the problems he could cause. She set about early in the semester to help him find a place for himself in that group. During a conference with him she learned that his main interests lay in two areas: aviation and hunting. In addition, he was well informed on current news events and politics. His attitudes toward school in general seemed to be good though he complained that he never had enough to do to keep him busy. Apparently his studies offered him no real challenge.

Upon learning these facts Jim's teacher became determined to help the boy overcome his difficulties. Over a period of many weeks, some of them trying, to say the least, she was able to give Jim opportunities to employ his special interests and talents.

It was he who aroused enthusiasm in the group for knowledge about current affairs. When he reported an event the others really listened. He lost his desire to create disturbances at these times because he was a recognized authority. When the group studied the Korean War, Jim naturally chose to work on the problems of the air forces. He became so interested in the project and did so well that he forgot to be obstreperous and demanding of the others. In working with them he found that others in his class had ideas and talent that he could benefit from. During the study of a unit on conservation, his interest in hunting was brought into the work of the classroom, and again he attacked the problems of the study with enthusiasm.

His teacher noticed, too, that Jim's attitude was improved in all other phases of classroom activity. She had been careful to provide him with a sufficient amount of research assignments and extra duties to keep him busy. She often sent him seeking reading materials for others in the class and it was not an uncommon sight to see Jim poring over data in the library to get just the needed bit of accurate information to solve a problem. He had found that he could learn something and could use his talents to a definite advantage. He discovered that there were many ways to gain recognition that did not involve mischief-making and dominating.

By the end of the year Jim's teacher noticed that he was being accepted more and more readily by the class. He retained some of his arrogant ways, but he was not the noisy troublemaker he had been. There was still room for improvement, but Jim was learning.

Had he not been given the opportunities that had benefited him so much, he might have continued in his heckling ways without real friends or recognition for his abilities—only a bad reputation to maintain. As it was, he had made use of his talents and interests, and with the help of an understanding teacher had begun to develop some of the characteristics of a useful citizen.

Photography was David's special talent. David did quite well in school but he could not see much point in all he had to go through to get a high school diploma when he knew that he wanted only to be a photographer after graduation. Nonetheless, he went through the motions, kept out of trouble, and managed to satisfy his parents and teachers with above-average grades.

In 9B, David was put into a general education class. For the first time in his school career he began to take some real interest in a class. The teacher had asked the class members to tell something about themselves and their hobbies. David brought his camera the next day in preparation for his talk. He was frightened at first because he had never shared his interests with these particular people before, but he soon lost his stage fright when he began to tell about his camera and to show some of his pictures. After the talk the children seemed friendlier somehow and some of them even asked to see more of his pictures. He went home that afternoon feeling quite satisfied with himself and the world in general.

David's teacher made a note of his interest in photography and determined to capitalize on it. She realized that she needed to use some techniques to pull David into group activities so that his school experience would become more meaningful to him. When some of the class members suggested that they might decorate the class bulletin board with pictures of everyone in the group, it was the teacher who suggested that David be the photographer. The class willingly agreed and went to work on plans for financing and carrying out the project.

There were other ways, too, throughout the year in which David's special talent for photography was brought into classroom work. He photographed civic buildings and housing conditions during a survey of the community that the class made. He used his flash attachment to record events at the Valentine's Day party. For the study of vocations he did a most commendable piece of work with a display and report on photography as a career.

The fact that David's interest in photography could be brought into the classroom made a great deal of difference to him and in his attitudes toward school, his classmates, and learning. Without his being aware of it, school assumed a new importance. For the first time his abilities and interests could be put to use, could be shared with others and admired by them. Thanks to his teacher, the remainder of his school days would be more meaningful and pleasant to him because through his photography he had been shown new ways of working. He had had new avenues of interest opened to him. He had received recognition from his peers. As a result he was better prepared to cope with what the next few years might bring him.

We have examined case studies of students whose special talents were utilized to advantage in classroom activities. Not only did these three students benefit by these experiences, but the entire group in each case was benefited in many ways. Some situations are not so dramatic as these nor of such direct import, but no matter how small the attempt to help a student adjust to a situation and become a contributing member of the group, it is well worth the effort. It can mean the difference between success and failure in his entire school career.

PUPILS FROM MINORITY GROUPS

One of the most difficult problems in human relations in the classroom is that of dealing with minority groups. The term "minority groups" covers a vast area in our present-day world, but for our purposes let us give it this interpretation: Minority groups consist of (1) children from families at the low socioeconomic level, often culturally deprived, and (2) those whose racial, national, or religious characteristics set them aside as being different from the majority of the group.

Students who fit into one or both of these categories can be found in virtually every classroom and their very existence presents a multitude of problems. Minority groups as defined above are a distinct asset to a class. Not only are they able to contribute to the groups, but they provide a real-life situation. Since learning to get along with others is one of the primary goals of teacher-pupil planning, a better proving ground cannot be found.

Before this phase of human relations in the classroom is discussed in more detail, let us list some assumptions that must necessarily be made. It is not reasonable to discuss here the problems of minority groups on a worldwide scale, but rather to confine them to a classroom situation. Before that can be done it must be assumed that:

1. the teacher who is using teacher-pupil planning techniques, and who desires to improve human relations in the class-

room, has herself a basic understanding of the problems of
minority groups.

2. the teacher is free from prejudice.

3. the teacher recognizes each pupil in the group as an individual possessing individual talents and faults, not group
talents and faults.

4. the teacher recognizes the fact that each student in the group
has preconceived ideas about others in the group, built up
by parents, peers, and community pressures, and that these
ideas are not readily cast aside.

5. the teacher and pupils are working together to dispel
prejudice, to bring about an understanding attitude toward
the problems of others, and to recognize the worth of the
individual.

Now that minority groups as they exist in the classroom have
been defined and the basic assumptions under which we must work
have been noted, let us look at several existing situations.

*The culturally deprived child from the lower socioeconomic
level.* As a ninth grader, Tom was small for his age group. His
clothing was old, ill-fitting, and rarely clean. His hair was shaggy,
his face drawn and pale. Boys and girls alike shunned him because
of his personal appearance. They shunned him, too, because his
scholastic abilities were limited. Tom had little to contribute to
the group. He came from a home where there were no books or
magazines or newspapers to read. For various reasons, his parents
were unable to provide him with any material possessions or educational experiences to enrich his life. His activities, in school and
out of school, were of little concern to them.

From the beginning of the year, Tom felt out of place and
soon sought the only defense he knew. He withdrew from contact
with other students whenever possible. When contact was necessary,
his face-saving device was belligerence. This attitude was displayed
to teachers and classmates alike. It was Tom's best defense against
being hurt.

What can be done to help a boy like Tom? Can he be helped
through the medium of classroom procedures? Is that the function
of the school or should the school concern itself solely with subject
matter and disregard the personality involved? One of Tom's
teachers decided that here was a boy to whom school work would
be of no value whatsoever until he made a place for himself among
his peers and regained his self-respect. Fortunately for Tom, she
took it upon herself to help him do just that. For a few days she
watched him very carefully and took no action except to be pleasant
and friendly. The rebuffs she received in response to her friendli-

ness could well have been misinterpreted had she not understood their meaning.

When groups were organized to work on the first project unit which was entitled "Orientation to our School," Tom could not decide which group he wanted to work with him. She seized upon this opportunity to place him in a working situation with some of the leading group members. She suggested that he work with the group investigating school sports. Tom agreed, though with obvious reluctance. While the effort was noble, the result was far from an unqualified success. Tom sat in silence most of the time the group was planning what to do and steadfastly refused to present any kind of report, giving the excuse that he had been unable to obtain any information. The teacher decided not to make an issue of the situation, but rather to try another approach when the opportunity presented itself.

While the class was in the midst of the next project unit, the group that Tom was spending his time with arranged to eat their lunches in the room one day in order to work on a display they had planned. When the teacher heard about this she made a special effort to urge Tom to bring his lunch and eat in the room with the others. He agreed to be there. The teacher brought her lunch that day and sat with the group around one of the tables. She directed the conversation toward Tom several times. The others in the group seemed to pay a little more attention to him than they had previously. When the chairman asked a question of the group, Tom volunteered an opinion. His teacher waited to see what would happen when they finished eating and went to work. To her surprise and pleasure Tom went to work on the display with an enthusiasm that had never before been apparent.

Did this one incident solve Tom's problem? Did his attitude and feeling of inferiority change overnight? No, of course not. But from this seemingly insignificant incident came the beginning of the solution to Tom's problems. From that time on he became a bit more willing to accept overtures of friendliness and was less likely to be belligerent. Through the medium of classroom procedure Tom was accepted for his individual worth. He might have found a place for himself in that school without the benefits of group planning and action, it is true, but the task was made easier for him through the help of an understanding teacher and a situation in which he was called upon to contribute his share in the planning and work.

The child from a minority racial group. Another typical situation concerning minority group members is that of having children from a different race in the minority in a classroom group.

It is a tremendous asset to have in a class a student or students who represent a race different from that of the majority. The situation brings its problems as well. Assuming as we did in point number 5 in the list of basic assumptions that "the teacher and pupils are working together to dispel prejudice, to bring about an understanding attitude toward the problems of others, and to recognize the worth of the individual," there is no better way to work on this problem than to have it confronting a classroom group in its daily activity.

There are many examples of worthwhile activities taking place in classrooms all over the nation that can be used here to illustrate how this problem of human relations is being handled. The following incidents are significant because they might have occurred in any school anywhere.

A seventh grade core class decided to devote part of the afternoon of Halloween to a party. When the suggestion was made by one of the group it was unanimously approved and a committee was appointed to work on arrangements. This kind of action is almost routine in a core class, but the difference in this case lies in the fact that the group was composed nearly equally of Negro pupils and white pupils. They had never attended school together before because of the geographic location of their homes and had never socialized together in any way. Only five weeks of the school term had passed when the proposal was made.

Naturally the teacher was apprehensive. She waited for the day to come when the deeply rooted prejudices of both groups would rise to the surface and the children would realize what they were planning. Ill feeling between the two groups was strong in the community and socializing was unheard of. The children of the two groups went their own ways for the most part. The teacher was earnestly seeking to dispel prejudice, but having had the group only five weeks she had not made a great deal of progress.

Plans for the party went on. Three days before the party the teacher was not surprised when an open conflict broke out. The committee reported that it needed more workers on the clean-up committee, so the president asked the group who would volunteer. A white boy stood up, laughed sarcastically, and said, "I nominate Melvin."

Melvin, who was a Negro, yelled out, "Yeah, you just would, wouldn't you?"

The entire class then entered into the discussion and the teacher could see that she would have to take over. She pretended to be surprised at the actions of the two boys and asked what was wrong. Melvin said he thought the whole party should be called off. When questioned further he blurted out, "From what I've been hearing when you're not around, they don't want to have a party with us!"

The meaning of his statement was all too clear. The teacher glanced over the group, pulled her chair up closer into the circle, and said, "Since there seems to be so much I don't know about, suppose you tell me just what is going on. Let's get this thing straightened out."

Gradually the story, obvious to the teacher from the beginning, was told. Each group aired its grievances cautiously, but enough was said that the teacher could go ahead and try to make amends. She carefully reviewed the problem for the group as she understood it. They did not want to be put into a situation where they would have to share each other's food, play games together, and perhaps practice social dancing together as the committee had planned. Then she put the question to the group: "What do you think we should do about this? Shall we call off the party or is there another way to handle it?"

Fortunately there was another way. Several leaders in the group came out with good suggestions as to how the problem could be solved and eventually the sense of fair play and good sportsmanship came to the fore. It was essential for that group to air its grievances before any workable solution could be found. After the hidden fears had been brought out into the open and discussed somewhat freely, everyone felt better.

This incident was an excellent lesson for everyone involved because it gave these pupils an insight into the problems of both groups. It was the beginning of improved human relations in that classroom and in countless unknown situations outside. The party was a success, because all the pupils worked together in a sincere effort to make it a success.

Alice Nishimura was a Japanese-American. She entered the tenth grade in a small Midwestern high school when her parents moved into the town to establish a small business. Alice was not too attractive and, while she was pleasant and polite when anyone approached her, she had nothing in common with the girls in her class. She was shy and withdrawn. The move into the new situation frightened Alice. Since she could not bring herself to make any friendly gestures and since she seemingly had little to offer, the other students virtually ignored her.

Her tenth grade core group entered into a group work project. As the groups were organizing Alice sat glued to her chair, afraid to volunteer for any part of the work. Finally her teacher suggested that Alice might like to work with a group of girls who were to investigate the homes and schools of France as a part of the problem "What is France contributing to the world today?"

Alice could not contribute much orally to the group. At first her fear of this new situation, plus the insecurity of her present life, made her afraid to speak out. The other girls were insensitive to the reasons for her withdrawal, but they assigned a part of the work dealing with the schools of France to her because they knew they should. The teacher helped her to find some resource material and Alice went to work eagerly, reading and taking notes.

When the groups met again the girls in Alice's group sat up and took notice. Here was a girl who could work. She had the best information of all; and while the others had barely begun reading through their mtaerial, Alice had exhausted her supply and needed other work to do. The teacher sat with the group and suggested that Alice might investigate another phase of the problem, or she might like to illustrate some of her findings for a bulletin board display. Alice decided to try some illustrative work in the form of charts that would simplify the statistical data she had. Since she had some artistic ability and was meticulous about her work, the charts were excellent and added a great deal to her report.

This girl, shy and insecure as she was, made a sincere effort to do good work. She knew that this was one way to gain the respect and admiration of the other pupils and her teachers. It was almost her only recourse at the time. Her teacher sensed what Alice was trying to do and helped her as much as possible, hoping that her academic success would provide the wedge that would allow her to secure a place for herself in other phases of school life. Gradually the others began to accept Alice. As she became more secure in the situation, she lost some of the shyness which had previously plagued her. She never was accepted as a member of any particular social group in her class, but the other students were friendly toward her and respected her abilities. In another situation, she might have spent all of her time in school just sitting alone, never having the opportunity to get acquainted with the other pupils because she was too shy to make the first move. As a result of group work and cooperative effort, however, she was able to make herself known to the others and gain the friendships and security she needed so badly.

Bill was a Jew. He had experienced almost every form of attack that prejudiced people in a non-Jewish community could inflict. Some of the youngsters in his neighborhood would not play with him. At the age of fourteen he knew what it was to be rejected because of his religion.

Fortunately for Bill he had two invaluable assets—educated, understanding parents and a magnificent intelligence. He was the most brilliant student his small Midwestern high school had ever had enrolled. In his leisure time at the age of twelve he read such books as *Les Misérables*. Bill was an avid philatelist and the envy of the other boys whose collections were much inferior to his. Bill's grades were always the highest possible and his knowledge on almost any topic, current or historical, was surprisingly complete and accurate.

Bill's father was a psychologist and had spent a great deal of time with his son, explaining his work and also training the boy to understand the situation he was in and the attitudes of other people toward him. Bill had an adult understanding of the problems that confronted Jews and other minority groups of the world. He was able to discuss these problems without malice or bitterness. He knew why some of his classmates shunned him and he knew how to cope with the problem intelligently.

One of Bill's particular friends, Dale, was not a Jew, but was handicapped physically by extremely poor vision. He also possessed superior intelligence and the two found many interests in common. Their core teacher became concerned about the fact that they never mingled with the others except in working situations in the classroom. There they could hold their own, but after class they were ignored by the others and were left to find what fun they could.

It was through Dale that Bill's teacher decided to work. She persuaded Dale to attend a school party and he in turn persuaded Bill to attend. They did not try to get dates, but decided to go stag. That night they both hung back when it came to dancing. Finally Bill decided to ask a girl to dance and fortunately she accepted. The girl was surprised to find that he was a good dancer. She soon passed the word along and when Bill asked some of the other girls to dance they were glad to accept.

That school dance, coupled with Bill's academic achievements, helped to erase the prejudice that his classmtaes felt toward him. The girls looked upon him with renewed interest and began to invite him to some of their private parties. The boys followed suit and began to seek him out more frequently. The teacher noticed that Bill was fiercely loyal to Dale and that both were included in social groups more and more often.

The fact that Bill was a Jew became less important to his classmates than the fact that he was a "regular guy." Through all these experiences, and by planning and working together, all of the students developed a better understanding of the problems they faced each day.

CONCLUSION

The problems cited here could arise in almost any classroom. There are many more problems not mentioned, all of them having individual characteristics and solutions because they concern individual human beings. Some of them are of greater magnitude than these, some are seemingly small and unimportant.

No matter what the scope of problems in human relations, none can be overlooked. Solutions cannot be found in one day or during one conference. Day by day, little by little, the fears that block the progress of pupils can be lessened or obliterated. The task requires patience, understanding, and a sincere desire to help pupils meet and solve the problems that face them in their everyday living.

Even though the results are not always successful, even though some methods bring defeat, a teacher should not be discouraged. The job of improving human relations is a teacher's direct responsibility. Real learning can be accomplished when pupils feel relaxed and secure.

Developing Leadership

W hen the teacher begins to share her role as the leader, one of the first problems is to discover with whom she can share leadership and how the eventual sharing can become diffused so as to develop all the potential leadership in the class.

Many fallacies have existed regarding the role of the leader. A few simple standards of leadership can be pointed out by the teacher. One step is to show what leadership in democratic processes is not:

1. Leadership is not forceful personality used to sway others.
2. Leadership is a series of skills that can be developed by many, not merely a favored few.
3. Leadership is not "pushing people around" to get them to follow the will of the leader.

Leadership has positive qualities:

1. Leadership is the ability to make each member of the group feel important and necessary.
2. Leadership is the skill of getting each member to suggest ideas and to comment on and consider the suggestions of others.
3. Leadership is the ability to help a group reach agreement through discussion and compromise.
4. Leadership is the skill of getting people to work together toward the common purpose, once agreement has been reached.
5. Leadership is the ability to help each member of a group have a satisfactory group experience.

At the beginning the teacher can give many helpful suggestions to the groups and leaders to get them off to a good start in an understanding of the leadership role. The following is one method that has been used with success at the beginning of the year:

Groups have been organized and leaders chosen. The first group meetings are about to be held. Their purpose is to plan a discussion of *Scholastic* magazine for the following week. The teacher has asked that groups begin to keep a record of meetings, plans, and evaluations. This will require choosing a recorder. She asks a group to volunteer to begin their meeting with others looking on, acting as a demonstration group for suggestions on how to get started. She first helps the leader with some simple parliamentary phraseology for handling the opening and the procedure toward planning. After the group is under way the teacher stops its work at a strategic point for discussion, suggestions, and questions. Thus, all leaders and group members feel more secure in knowing how to begin.

Following the first meetings and frequently thereafter it is a good plan for leaders to have meetings for discussing and sharing problems and experiences. The teacher can take charge of these meetings and ask leaders to present problems. They do so willingly, bringing up such questions as these:

"Two girls in my group talk about their boyfriends part of the time."

"John won't participate. He just fools around and bothers others."

"I don't like to have the kids in my group think that just because I am the leader I am trying to throw my weight around. How can I get them to cooperate without being bossy?"

The teacher facilitates the discussion by asking such questions as:

"Anyone else have this problem? What did you do about it?"

"What makes John act this way? Is there anything we can do to help him?"

"What things did you discover worked well with your group?"

An informal discussion like this one will often give the leaders more confidence and help them solve many problems in group relationships.

Not only the selected leaders of organized groups can be of help to the teacher and the class. The sociogram showing the friendship pattern is of no value if it is only a document to be filed away, but it can become a very valuable tool in the hands of a teacher who will make use of the strong interpersonal relationships among her students. Without ever referring openly to the questionnaire from which the sociogram is made, the teacher begins to use the information gained for the improvement of class relations and output. One group showing up in the sociogram that she will surely make use of is the leader group. Teachers using sociometric material have discovered that the true leaders of the class are often entirely different from those the teacher would pick for leadership. The "bright" student, who always has his hand in the air and is the first to volunteer to do errands for the teacher, is seldom the chosen leader of the class.

Once the leaders have been spotted, there are many services they can perform for the class. In one class of seventeen boys and thirteen girls a group of four boy leaders was asked to help with the discipline and human relations problems of the class. Every other boy in the room admired one or more of these four boys and wished to be included in their crowd. Three other boys in the class also had marked leadership influence and were chosen as friends and, by many, as those with whom they liked best to work. Two very insecure boys had violent tempers and aggressive, quarreling tendencies. Two others withdrew in shyness, taking no part in activities of the class. Another insecure lad would go to any extreme to get attention from the boys in the clique. Another leader had his close friends outside the class; he was a red-headed, good-humored extrovert who wielded both good and bad influence.

The teacher called together the most sought-after boys, the ones who had been chosen by twelve or more as friends. She asked them if they had any ideas about how the class could work better together. She told them that they seemed to be more self-confident than others and that perhaps there was some way they could help the class as a whole. The response was heartening and wholehearted. They talked frankly about various class members and how and why they were problems in a class. The teacher went into the psychological implications of behavior somewhat, and she told the boys that everyone works better and acts better in a situation where he feels accepted and at ease. Such comments as these showed remarkable insight on the part of these boys:

"I think Randy acts that way because he is trying to get attention. His older brother was a big wheel in football, and the family likes him better than Randy."

"Wayne is smaller than any of the rest of us kids. He probably feels funny when he is around us. He doesn't have very good clothes either."

"Ken always has been that way. He used to fight with all the kids in grade school. He lives with his grandmother because his parents are divorced. Maybe that's why he is so mean."

The teacher asked them if there was anything they could do for the insecure ones which would help them feel more a part of the class. They suggested that they might just say a friendly "hi" in the morning to some who were more or less ignored. They said that everyone should surely be included when committee choices were being made. They suggested some seating changes and group changes. They did not overdo their plans, but rather, in somewhat typical masculine fashion, they recognized what was to be done and did it.

The effect on the class was very satisfactory. The complete isolate was chosen by the extrovert a few days later for his committee. The expression of surprise and pleasure on Wayne's face upon being chosen was one the teacher will not soon forget. The rejected ones can, and indeed must, be accepted by the teacher; but nothing can be more satisfying to a shy adolescent than being accepted by his peers.

It will be noted that the teacher did not invest any of these people with responsibilities beyond their ability. She did not turn the problems over to them but rather asked them for their help. Students will often say to the teacher, " I think Ken is doing better," with a feeling of pride in a class accomplishment. The teacher is also careful not to exploit leadership and thus endanger the leader's status with his group.

Often we are called upon by school or community to sell ideas or material things. Here the teacher who has had difficulty in selling her quota of Christmas seals, for example, will find a class leader doing the task in no time.

Frequent discussions and sociodramas showing the role of the leader are helpful. Leadership has a way of changing with different situations, and it is helpful to a class to know that everyone finds himself in a position of leadership at some time and that the role is not reserved for a chosen few. Sometimes group leaders feel that too much is expected of them by other members of their group. Group-leader conferences, class evaluation by the leaders, and other devices for solving problems may be put into use.

As they become more aware of analyzing group processes, students are able to give many suggestions for the development of better leadership. In one class that had worked together for eight months a questionnaire on leadership brought evidence of a very analytical attitude toward the role. This questionnaire, introduced informally by the teacher, was as follows:

1. What makes a good leader?
2. How can we help solve the problems of leaders?
3. What can we do to develop leaders?

Summary of this questionnaire follows. No effort has been made to reword students' comments.

1. *What makes a good leader?* (Answers seemed to divide themselves into qualities and skills.)

Qualities

Get along with people	Honest
Be friendly	Considerate of others
Good personality	Have a "way" with people
Initiative	Good disposition
Neat and clean	Can take criticism easily
Likeable	Like everyone
Good judgment	Be understanding
Cool headed	Sense of humor
Easy to get along with	Poise
Not shy	Good speaker
Be willing to do certain things	Willing to work
Have friends	Serious
Courteous	Kind
Dependable	Pleasant
Control temper	Helpful

Skills

Know how to run a business meeting
Get people to work for and with the group
Keep the group quiet
Know what his group is doing and how they are doing it
Help the group
Get an idea across
Lead in a problem
Use good language
Handle the group
Know what he is doing
Figure out what to do to help the whole group
Make the right decisions
Keep the spirits high
Know how to associate with people
People want to agree with him
Help group get to work rapidly
Help group get along with one another
Keep up the morale of the group
Understand people
Keep the group interested in the same things
Get them to cooperate
Follow directions
Understand the qualifications of leadership
Know what every person is like

Work mentally with the group instead of physically
Make people want to work
Do well in your work
Have good ideas
Have some control over people
Be liked by people
Know correct business meeting terms
Help carry on good and thorough discussion
Know how to please people
Make everyone feel that he wants to work
Have schedule planned
Make things interesting
Control your feelings
Participate
Watch feelings of others

2. *How can we help solve the problems of leaders?*

Be with the group all the time, not keep leaving. Not talk about everything but work.

Arrange seating. Put the people who like to talk closer together so they won't have to shout. (Note how this suggestion differs from the average teacher's approach to the same problem!)

Stay with the group. Do not run off when the group is discussing something important.

Sit down and talk it out.

Assign duties.

Have an intermission.

Bear down when they won't do things.

We talk about our problems openly. Sometimes we think about them and then each give our own opinions.

Talk over our problems and find some kind of solution.

Discuss the problem until it is solved.

Talk about leadership.

Share in work equally.

Give all a fair chance in making choices.

Everyone go halfway in helping to solve problems.

Give everyone who hasn't had the responsibility a chance to be a leader.

Do not think just because you are a leader that you are better than anyone else.

Don't laugh at or make fun of anyone who makes a mistake. Let him do the best he can so that he feels he has accomplished something.

When a person has an idea, don't tell him he is stupid or
crazy. Listen to his whole idea and say maybe we could
use it.
Want to do things for people.
Get along with the teacher. Have her help you.
Do not act stuck-up.
All participate in giving helpful suggestions.
Set up goals; write them out.
More discussions and meetings.
Observe other groups and leaders.
Always ask advice of the group on important problems.
Always do what is best for the whole group.

3. *What can we do to develop leaders?*

Practice in our groups. Learn from others.
Take opportunities to lead in discussions.
Observe the presidents of the class.
Cooperate.
Have leaders have more talks with the teacher, and have the
students talk with the teacher without the leaders.

The teacher used the results of this questionnaire for a discussion
with the class. In addition to the points above, she read some of the
discussions like the following, deleting actual names, of course:

"There are several good leaders in our class. They are Lois D.,
Ellen S., Larry J., and Bill W. All of these people have these qualities: They cooperate with the group and class; they are willing to
take responsibility, and I have never seen them grumpy or unkind."

One excellent girl leader evaluated another thus:

"Judy J. contributes a lot to the class and goes ahead and does
things when other people don't. She is polite and nice. She gets
along with people very well. She has good ideas and people seem
to work for her."

A boy who was a serious behavior problem throughout the year
had this to say about one of the girl leaders:

"I think Sandra T. was the best leader I have ever worked
with and probably ever will. When I needed help Sandra was
always the one to help. I think I should credit her for getting
the good mark I got at the end of the first semester, and if Sandra
gets an A I think she fully deserves it in more ways than just her
school work. I think she has the best disposition of any person
I have ever seen. I recommend Sandra for helping anybody who
really needs help in any project."

Often pupils have said: "At some time every member of our

class has been a leader." Such comments seem to indicate an appreciation of the more subtle phases of leadership and recognition of the limitless possibilities of diffusion of leadership in democratic processes.

CHAPTER 9

The Role of the Teacher

The part the teacher plays in learning experience influences to a great extent the success of the undertaking. A music teacher can help her pupils enjoy singing together even though some of them can hardly carry a tune. Another teacher could cause them to hate the words "music class" if her own attitude were negative toward them and their work. The teacher sets the stage. What transpires can be a direct result of her behavior patterns and philosophy. These facts are especially important to a teacher who wants teacher-pupil planning to succeed in her classes.

Though many people believe that the teacher has an easy task when she lets pupils help in planning and carrying out activities, this is far from the truth. The success or failure of the venture depends upon the skill of the teacher, and the task is exacting. Perhaps the first thing to consider regarding the role of the teacher is the question of her philosophy and aims.

GOALS

Each teacher needs to establish goals for herself. She should ask herself, "What am I trying to do? What are my beliefs? Why do I believe these things?" It would be well to write out the answers to these questions; sometimes it is surprising to see one's beliefs in writing—surprising and revealing.

Goals for a teacher who believes in teacher-pupil planning are understandably different from those of a teacher who places major emphasis on subject matter. They are probably broader in scope, including some aims that were not considered important in the past. Below are the goals that we have set for ourselves. These might be suitable goals for almost any teacher in any situation.

They do apply particularly, however, to teachers who are using teacher-pupil planning.

I. To help pupils develop skills in working with others.

II. To help pupils develop skills in identifying and solving problems that are pertinent to their everyday lives.

III. To help pupils develop good work and study habits.

IV. To help pupils develop skills in communication.
    A. Improve ability to write, incorporating clear thought as well as good word usage, punctuation, sentence structure, and spelling.
    B. Improve silent reading for comprehension.
    C. Improve oral reading.
    D. Improve speech through reports and discussions, with attention to clear thinking, correct word usage, and correct pronunciation.

V. To help pupils develop social skills.

VI. To help pupils improve attitudes, increase appreciation for cultural growth, and develop worthy ideals.

VII. To help pupils gain an understanding of and an appreciation for the peoples and problems of the world.

VIII. To help pupils gain skill in constructive evaluation.

IX. To help pupils use all possible resources for learning.

X. To help pupils increase knowledge of factual material.

XI. To help pupils practice democratic living in order to develop an understanding of democratic rights and responsibilities.

XII. To learn to know our pupils.

XIII. To give pupils the satisfaction and feeling of responsibility that comes from helping with the planning.

RESPONSIBILITIES

Just as pupils learn through teacher-pupil planning that responsibility accompanies freedom, so must teachers realize that certain obligations are hers when she takes upon herself the task of planning with pupils. Much criticism has been leveled at modern teaching methods, some of it justly. There are teachers who try teacher-pupil planning in all sincerity but who fail through lack of experience and knowledge. And there are teachers who seize upon these methods as an easy way out of a hard job, allowing their pupils to create chaos in the classroom. There are others, however, who have been really successful in this work. If more teachers would accept the responsibilities that are so much a part of trying new teaching methods and would strive conscientiously to attain the goals they set for themselves, criticism would be at a minimum.

First, a teacher has a responsibility to her pupils. It is up to her to help them in every way she can to become better informed and to learn the ways of democratic living. Also it is her task to supplement these skills with improved social skills, attitudes, and appreciations. She is the one who is in the position to stimulate this growth in her pupils.

Second, a teacher has responsibilities regarding her colleagues. She cannot hope to prepare her pupils in all respects for the "next grade"—that is an impossibility. She should, however, take into consideration what is ahead of her students and plan with them accordingly. In addition, a teacher who uses teacher-planning will probably find that her pupils need to use other rooms at different times to work, practice, study, and do research. She must be extremely careful to be considerate of other teachers and their situations to avoid conflict.

Third, a teacher has responsibilities to her administrators. Perhaps she has been encouraged to try teacher-pupil planning by her administrators, perhaps she has badgered them into letting her try it, perhaps she is doing it in spite of them. In any case she has an ethical responsibility to work within certain bounds so that she is not the perpetrator of serious misunderstandings. She also has the responsibility of carrying out the policies set up and practiced by the school system that employs her.

Fourth, a teacher has certain responsibilities to the parents of her pupils. Many parents have not been given the opportunity to understand the purposes and reasons for what transpires in the classes their children attend. It is up to the teacher to explain very carefully what she is trying to do (another reason for being sure of her philosophy) and to help parents understand her procedures. Parents have every right to know what is happening to their children and if some of them become irate it is often, unfortunately, with just cause. No parents could condemn a teacher's sincere effort to help their child. No teacher has the right to resent their inquiries; indeed, they should be welcomed. It is a teacher's responsibility to interpret educational methods and to cooperate with the parents of her pupils.

WHAT QUALITIES ARE NEEDED?

The discussion thus far might frighten teachers away from teacher-pupil planning because it sounds much too demanding. Actually it is far from that. It is the most enjoyable way of teaching possible, but it takes one who can carry a big load and enjoy herself to make a success of it. A sense of humor is a valuable asset to any teacher, but particularly to the core-type teacher. Some days everything goes wrong and the only possible way to survive is to laugh it off and think of better ways for tomorrow.

Add to a sense of humor an imaginative spirit and you have another ingredient that helps to make up a good teacher. When one is planning and working with pupils, ideas sometimes have to be supplied by the more mature mind to keep things going. Patience, of course, is always needed in teaching. Enthusiasm, too, is a great asset. When pupils sense that the teacher is enthusiastic about what is being planned, they are much more enthusiastic themselves.

Many questions have been raised about discipline in core-type classes. The point cannot be overlooked, but it should not be overstressed either. It is an unavoidable fact that pupils will misbehave sometimes in spite of everything anyone can do. Ideally, if we are doing a really superior job of teacher-pupil planning—involving all the pupils, helping them to enjoy a real learning experience—we should have little or no trouble with mischief-makers. It is true that there are not too many real problems of discipline when students have a share in the planning, and when problems do come up the group can be called upon for solutions. There are times, though, when one or two students, or perhaps the whole group, fail to carry out their responsibilities or behave in such a way as to make it impossible for the others to work. Then the teacher must take action to improve the situation. Teacher-pupil planning does not mean that pupils may do exactly as they please at all times. It cannot succeed with a laissez-faire attitude on the part of the teacher. A teacher cannot tolerate excessive noise and confusion. It is her job to create an atmosphere where real learning can take place. She can do that by being firm, but always understanding.

More important than any other quality is one we shall call "selflessness." Teacher-pupil planning cannot succeed with a domineering, self-centered, demanding teacher. A teacher must be well-informed, but she cannot supply all the answers. She must be willing to say, "I don't know, either, but let's find out." A teacher must constantly be alert to what is going on. She will never find time to do records or look over reports during a class if she is really working with her pupils. These things have to come later—after school or on the weekend. She must take her place as a participating member of the group, just as the pupils do, and she must always be willing to have her suggestions bypassed in favor of others. If that means that her pupils make mistakes, then she must help them to profit by their mistakes, again as a member of the group. She must be able to give and take as others do and yet know when to step in if help is needed, without demands and without dictatorial tactics.

PERSONAL RELATIONSHIPS WITH PUPILS

Chapter 2 introduced some methods of getting acquainted; actually the process never ends. The personal relationships between teachers and pupils and between pupils and pupils become cemented with heightened interest, increased understanding, and friendly acceptance. The very nature of the activities presupposes the development of a friendly spirit of cooperation. To her pupils the teacher becomes more than the head of the classroom, the adult authority. She becomes a consultant, an adviser, a confidante, a friend.

The teacher as a consultant. In discussing selflessness we mentioned that a teacher must be well informed but that she cannot supply all the answers. The definition of a consultant applies to a teacher—an expert on a given matter. She must be an expert in her field or she could not qualify for her job. Her students look to her for answers to their questions and solutions to their problems. A good teacher will help her students find the answers and solutions, not provide them. She acts as a consultant to her students, always ready with suggestions and ideas. They learn quickly that she has good suggestions and ideas and is willing to help them. They also learn that she will not insist that things be done her way only, but will be willing to listen to their ideas and prod them gently toward achieving their goals.

The teacher as an adviser and confidante. A teacher who spends two or three hours a day working with her pupils naturally has the opportunity to learn things about them that perhaps no other person in the school system can. She does not need to invite them in for a conference or to seek their confidence. They are already there and she has time to talk with them. The atmosphere for confidence is right, too, if she is doing a good job. Many times pupils will say things in an easy, relaxed working situation that will give a teacher a clue to their problems in other classes or outside of school. By indirect counseling a teacher can do a great deal to mold attitudes and character as little things come up in day-to-day relationships. Sometimes pupils will ask for help directly if they feel that they can trust their teacher.

She is in a position then to provide real help because she knows her pupils. Because of her close personal relationships with them she understands their motives, their drives, their aggressions, and their shortcomings. The possibilities for really helping her pupils are limitless in such a situation. Relationships like these are built only when confidence and trust have been well established. That takes time and effort and strict adherence to a policy of honesty and sincerity.

The teacher as a friend. A teacher might shy away from the idea of developing friendships with pupils because she feels she would lose their respect. Perhaps she is afraid to lower that imaginary line which exists between pupils and teachers to keep both in their respective places. Proceeding cautiously in this matter is wise; only the situation and the persons involved can determine how far the line can be lowered.

The behavior patterns we have been discussing will promote friendships between teachers and pupils, and when propertly handled that can be most desirable. A friend is a person who can be counted on to stand by, regardless of what happens. When pupils come to feel that way about their teacher they gain security in their work and in their relationships with others. Serving as a consultant, becoming an adviser and confidante, naturally lead to more friendly relations. A teacher can have a real influence on her pupils, and her sincere interest in their problems and activities gives them a satisfaction they might not get elsewhere. She does not have to lose her status or her pupils' respect to be friends with them. She earns their respect and strengthens her status with her friendly attitude.

The following quotations illustrate qualities students seem to value in their teachers:

"I like the democratic way of doing things. Our teacher has taken an interest in everyone. She gives us a lot of individual attention."

"I like this class and all the kids and the teacher especially because she doesn't get mad and yell at us like our teacher did last year."

"A teacher should have a sense of humor and a sense of understanding. She should work with us and offer us help. She should get along with everybody."

"This class is good because we can make our own decisions and our teacher has time to explain our work to us."

"You can talk more freely to the teacher. The teacher and the kids listen to your opinions. You have a right to say what you think."

"The advantages of the core class are many. I think we get to know our classmates better and really understand their problems. We have more chance for leadership and to express our own ideas. I feel that I know you a lot better than I have ever known any of my other teachers."

"In the past year I have learned more than I have since I have been in junior high. School is not based wholly on subject matter, but on personality, leadership, getting along with others, manners, and cooperation. To me these things are more important than subject matter, and I have learned a great deal about them in our G. E.

class. Having Miss ——— as a teacher has been wonderful. She is easy to get along with and understands people, and I think if we didn't have her for a teacher I wouldn't have felt as I do about the class, for I think she has a lot to do with the success of the class."

"Our teacher is more like a friend than a teacher. We can have fun with her, but she understands our problems, too. She will be a consultant when we need help, but she will let us find things out for ourselves, too."

SUMMARY

The part that the teacher plays is of the utmost importance. She needs to determine her goals and to try sincerely to achieve these goals. She has responsibilities to her pupils, to her colleagues, to the administration, and to the parents of her pupils. A teacher who works with teacher-pupil planning needs to have a sense of humor, an imaginative spirit, and enthusiasm for her work. She needs to be able to handle discipline problems with firmness and understanding. Forgetting herself, she should be able to work with her students as a participating member of the group, always willing to give and take as the situation demands. She will find that through knowing her students well, she will come to serve as a consultant, an adviser, a confidante, and ultimately become a friend. The teacher who really wants to make a success of her work in teacher-pupil planning will find it an exacting task, but one that brings a great deal of satisfaction.

CHAPTER 10

External Problems in Teacher-Pupil Planning

A discussion of the techniques and problems involved in teacher-pupil planning would not be complete without some mention of the various situations that often exist for a teacher outside her classroom. Chapter 9 dealt briefly with the responsibilities that a teacher has to her colleagues. Let us look further into this matter.

Very often a core teacher has a selling job to do. Since her approach in the classroom is different from that of most other teachers she is likely to be a target for criticism, set apart from her colleagues. One of the teacher's goals previously expressed is to help pupils develop skills in working with one another. As an adult she needs to make a special effort to keep her relationships harmonious even with those who may differ sharply in philosophy.

Other teachers on a faculty are sometimes resentful of the core program in a school, particularly when it is first introduced. They feel as though they are pushed into the background because so much emphasis and attention is given to developing the new idea. Their work has been satisfactory over the years. Suddenly they develop a sense of insecurity because their well-established methods are no longer in vogue. It is only natural that they should look critically at the new program and the people involved in it.

The more established teacher often has good reason to be critical because unfortunately some core teachers place themselves in a select group, creating the impression that they should be granted special consideration. The intelligent, sensitive core teacher will be very careful not to assume this attitude, but instead to find a place for herself in the existing situation without causing undue friction. She can do this fairly easily if she makes an effort to be considerate of other teachers, their feelings and their problems.

Teachers became irritated more by having core classes around than for any other reason. They do not like to have their classes interrupted by a noisy committee making its way down the hall in the middle of a class. They do not like to have pupils excused from their classes to go to the mayor's office or to the downtown library for the morning. They are annoyed when a group uses any available room in the building for its various activities, and they particularly dislike being put out of their own rooms during their one free period. And why wouldn't they object?

Common sense should tell any teacher that these seemingly minor annoyances can be avoided. Pupils can learn that they must not create disturbances while moving from place to place in the building. Teachers can help students plan their activities so that the whole school does not suffer an inconvenience. It takes only a little thought and consideration from others to keep from being a disrupting element. Teacher-pupil planning will then be much more readily accepted.

Occasionally more serious problems arise. Some teachers are firmly opposed to anything different, regardless of its merits. They will not make any effort to understand; they will not even wait to see whether the new ideas will be successful. They might even try to sabotage the program in many ways. It takes skill to work with these persons without sacrificing the principles one believes in. Since one must work with them for the good of all concerned, a maximum amount of effort must be expended to keep relationships harmonious.

Fortunately the majority of a teacher's co-workers outside the core program are cooperative and sympathetic. Even though they may look dubiously upon the philosophy and activities involved, they will do what they can to be helpful. The wise core teacher will seek their help and take advantage of their interest, experience, and knowledge.

A core teacher meets problems in working with other core teachers, too. No two people can operate exactly alike in any situation. Each core teacher has her own ideas about how to deal with teacher-pupil planning. Each teacher should be free to experiment and find suitable ways. One can readily see, though, that this method of operation can lead to friction among those involved and criticism from others not directly concerned. In addition to the problems involved in methodology there are problems in personal relationships to deal with. Core teachers do not differ from other human beings; a core teacher often finds that there are serious differences to be resolved among those who share the same philosophy.

TEACHER-ADMINISTRATOR RELATIONSHIPS

In common with all humanity the core teacher, or any teacher who is deviating from the generally accepted methods of teaching, needs the security of administrative approval, understanding, and leadership. Not one of us can operate independently in these fields, which involve all the subtleties of human relationships. Some of the problems mentioned earlier in the chapter have the beginnings of a solution in the attitudes and actions of the administrative leader.

First of all, the administrator must be philosophically in sympathy with the program and the implementation of teacher-pupil planning methods. He must believe sincerely that the school's purpose is to afford the best possible opportunities for the development of the whole child and that the best possible methods may not yet have been found. His philosophy must be positive, not negative. It must be constant, for ambivalence leads to lack of security in teachers that undoubtedly communicates itself eventually to students. If the administrator accepts the philosophy that leads to the use of teacher-pupil planning methods, he will establish in his school a policy of freedom to experiment with new methods and ideas. The type of in-service training program which is a necessary means to any effective program in a school is especially important here, and the administrator must provide the positive and enthusiastic leadership that leads to real progress and understanding among the members of a school staff.

To extend the leadership necessary in such an ongoing program, the administrator must be well informed about current educational trends. He will be alert to new ideas, and he will know where interesting and meaningful practices are taking place. He will be not merely grudgingly willing, but actually eager, to give teachers opportunities for stimulation and improvement. Staff members will be encouraged to exchange materials and information—a professional library is indicated here—and he should schedule teachers with common problems in such a way that they will have time to get together for an exchange of ideas. The administrator, too, will be available for such meetings, for the problems of the school are his problems.

In addition to these in-school activities, the leader-administrator will facilitate attendance at meetings and conferences and encourage visits to other school programs. Some administrators object to a teacher's being away from school for a day, saying that teachers are hired to be in the classroom and that they are costing the school board money. Such an attitude shows a lack of understanding that teachers need and benefit immeasurably by such experiences, and that the results in good morale and improved classroom practices far outweigh any disadvantages of such opportunities. Only recently has the educational world recognized that teachers, as well as administrators, need to grow professionally.

The administrator will strive for good relations with individual teachers. He will find time to talk over problems with them, he will be ready to give praise when deserved and encouragement when needed. He will, in short, have the human approach to the program.

These requirements of an administrator are certainly not limited to a teacher-pupil planning program, for they are desirable in any case. The active support, however, is vital here, for many times the administrator is called upon to interpret the program to his staff and to the community as well. Parents are entitled and eager to know what is happening to their children in school. They can also be fine resources in such a program; many are intensely interested in the philosophical and psychological thinking that leads to new educational trends.

The core teacher has a distinct obligation to the administrator who has shown good faith and exercised wise leadership. In addition to practicing the ethics of the teaching profession, she has some unique rules to follow. If she lacked enthusiasm, she would not be a core teacher, but she should never allow it to run away with her to the extent of monopolizing valuable time with endless accounts of "what my class did today." She must learn to omit the trivialities and yet be alert to the significant and overall experiences. In his interpretation of the program, the principal will need to know much about the methods and results of work in a core class, and it takes some skill on the part of the teacher to assemble significant data for him to use. She should share with him evidences of significant results in learning, personality changes, attitude changes, and the like.

Undoubtedly, the core group will have an established policy of notifying the office of any unusual activities that take students out of the building or bring guests into it. The teacher should be considerate enough to do nothing that will embarrass the principal if he should have to make any explanations. There are many other activities in the school, and the principal has obligations to all.

Such problems will be minimized if the administrator opens the channels of communication between himself and teachers and among teachers themselves. He must play an active and diversified role in any effective program of teacher-pupil planning.

SUMMARY

A teacher engaged in teacher-pupil planning needs to make a special effort to keep her relations harmonious even with those who may differ sharply in philosophy. Other teachers feel antagonistic toward a new program at times because they feel that they are being pushed into the background. Core teachers need to be especially careful not to allow their students to become a disturbing influence. They need to take care that they do not expect special privileges.

In working with other teachers directly connected with the program, a core teacher has to be willing to cooperate with others, listen to their opinions, and try to give and take as the situation demands. The success of the entire program depends upon her knowledge of her work, her professional attitudes, and her clarity of thinking in relation to her actions and her philosophy.

Administrators should give active professional leadership to the core program. They should be available for conferences with groups or individuals. They should provide direction for in-service training programs, in which they help the staff to interpret educational trends. They should encourage attendance at conferences and visits to other schools. They should act as interpreters of the program to staff and community.

Core teachers for their part should recognize the many demands on the time of an administrator and should not waste time on trivialities. They should observe rules of the school, especially as to policies regarding field trips and out-of-schoolroom activities. They should be alert to significant developments that will keep their administrator informed on the progress of the program and the people involved in it.

CHAPTER 11

Teacher-Pupil Planning in the World Scene

The heritage of the children of the United States has its origin in the tenets of individual freedom. The essence of a democracy is recognition of the worth of each of its citizens and his responsibility for its perpetuation. Since the year 1776, marking the signing of the Declaration of Independence, the American people have sought ways to educate their children so that the struggle for freedom from oppression would not have been in vain, so that the democratic way of life would be preserved.

This nation faces many problems, foreign and domestic, but it persists in its determination to preserve this democratic society. What we fail to recognize is that in the nation's schools, the methods employed to teach our children the ways of democracy are often, in themselves, undemocratic. Here, in our children, lies the future of the society we treasure. We cannot expect them to develop into good citizens, to have faith in our beliefs, and to assume their responsibilities simply by attempting to fill them with knowledge about our form of government and their heritage and by telling them that it is right and good.

They must be given the opportunity to live and participate in a democratic situation; they must experience the process and discover for themselves its strengths and weaknesses before they can truly appreciate its worth and really understand its meaning. All research concerning the learning process tells us that we learn through experience. True understanding and appreciation do not evolve unless the learner participates in the process of learning.

The school classroom holds the greatest hope for the preservation of democracy. The methods we have described in this book can help children to become informed, participating citizens in our democratic society. This is the school's primary function. Teacher-pupil planning can help the individual child to recognize problems, to plan an attack, to work out that plan, to share his finding with others, and to evaluate his efforts. Skill in this process, coupled with the basic skills and knowledge needed to create an informed citizen, can form a pattern for living and facing the realities everyone must face.

These procedures can give students practice in participating with others to arrive at decisions based on research, thought, and fact. As he matures, he will be more aware of his own problems and those of society and will be better prepared to participate in their solutions. Industry has long sought people who could get along with others and work cooperatively with fellow employees for the good of the whole. Science needs teams of people who can pool their resources to move ahead to still greater inventions, still-sought-for discoveries. In the interest of humanity there is a critical need for those with deep understanding, deep faith, and convictions, who can teach and lead the people of this nation and the world to practice the ideals of freedom, equality, and peace.

A portion of the Preamble to the Charter of the United Nations Organization and some important comments are cited here to illustrate the goals which peace-loving nations strive for:

To save succeeding generations from the scourge of war;
To reaffirm faith in fundamental human rights;
To establish conditions under which justice and respect for . . . international law can be maintained;
To promote social progress and better standards of life.

Furthermore, it affirms that in order to gain these ends, the Peoples of the United Nations are determined to practice tolerance, to live in peace as good neighbors, to unite to maintain peace and security, to ensure that armed forces shall not be used except in the common interest, and to employ international machinery for the social and economic betterment of all peoples.

One striking feature of the Preamble may be noticed. The covenants of the League of Nations and many other international documents begin with the phrase "The high contracting parties," but the Preamble, like the Constitution of the United States, speaks in the name of the peoples.[1]

This document illustrates vividly how much the world needs citizens who have the attributes necessary for carrying out these goals and aims. It is at the classroom level that these citizens can be cultivated and nurtured. Helping children to understand and

[1] *Guide to the United Nations Charter*, U.N. Department of Public Information, 1950.

practice democratic principles can be the greatest contribution teachers can make to the world, for it is with these children that the fate of mankind rests.

We feel that teacher-pupil planning in its broadest concept and application can help to fulfill this need, which has been variously expressed in the following letters to the authors from leaders in American life:

EDUCATION SPEAKS

I believe that the most urgent problem in education today is that of method. The method that we have inherited from the past fails primarily because it does not include the learner; therefore if the learner becomes involved at all, it is by accident.

It is difficult to see how the learner can be involved in what is to be learned without teacher-pupil planning. It is also hard to see how democracy can be promoted without the inclusion and involvement of everyone. Efforts to broaden the use of teacher-pupil planning are bound to be in the right direction. Those who practice democratic method and share their experiences through writing need and deserve the enthusiastic support of all of us who care about the democratic way of life.

> *Earl C. Kelley*
> *Professor, Secondary Education*
> *Wayne State University*
> *Detroit, Michigan*

We Americans must recognize in all humility that the American scene represents the "drawing board" for future democratic living. Universal suffrage, freedom of speech and religion and self-government grow out of literacy education plus democratic practices in the school and classroom. Experiences in teacher-pupil planning, committee work, directing class sessions and self-evaluation are essential to the development of creative American citizens.

> *G. Robert Koopman*
> *Associate Superintendent,*
> *Michigan Department of Public Instruction*
> *Lansing, Michigan*

Democracy cannot be taught. To become an effective way of living it must be practiced day in and day out from kindergarten through the university.

> *Paul J. Misner*
> *Superintendent,*
> *The Public Schools of Glencoe*
> *Glencoe, Illinois*

For the past 180 years, this country has enjoyed the illimitable blessings of democracy without much awareness of the factors which enable it to function as a form of government and as a way of living. There has been relatively little effort to analyze it and to develop recognition of the responsibilities and obligations of freedom. But with the inevitable changes and challenges which are being brought about by the atom and by the closer relationships of all parts of the world, it is imperative that more attention be given to the understanding and the learning of democratic living. It is essential that we in the schools constantly seek more ways to advance the cause of democracy by teaching and practicing its principles. We must plan definitely for the use of the skills involved. While we must cause children to acquire knowledge, we must also teach them citizenship. Democracy is worth all our best efforts, lest apathy let it drain away.

> *Martha Shull*
> *President* (1956-57)
> *National Education Association*
> *Washington, D.C.*

Democracy must become more than a nice word and it must mean more than the right to vote and the freedom to do as we please. If it is to survive, we must continually strive in our schools to teach our children something more than the usual catch phrases and clichés. Democracy is a live, growing concept and it no longer can be limited to a few countries but must demonstrate its ability to solve the world's most pressing problems for all mankind, such as the problems of war, of hunger, and of human dignity.

> *John H. Furbay*
> *Director, Air World Education*
> *New York, New York*

Democracy, both as a political and economic system and as a way of life, rests on the participation of the individual in the solution of all problems that concern the group. The complexities of group living require more than good will for the solution of problems—there must also be experience and technique. Modern schools have accepted the value that children should be allowed responsibility and self-control as rapidly as, and to the extent that, they evidence a sufficient maturity for it. Modern schools give children opportunities for participtaion in the determination of plans and in the making of choices. Such experiences are a part of a design intended to give children practice in ways of behaving in a democracy.

> *Willard C. Olson*
> *Child Development*
> *D. C. Heath and Company*
> *Boston, Massachusetts,* 1949

LABOR SPEAKS

Democracy is not something given, it is something achieved. It cannot be equated with voting rights in periodic elections. It is a highly-evolved way of living with oneself and with one's fellows.

Democracy is not an instinctive order. Since it is predicated not so much upon human freedom as upon the right use of human freedom, it is not easily won and not easily maintained. Anarchy or some form of tyranny has been a more common historical response to the problem of organizing human communities.

A democratic society, then, raises the most complex problems of responsibility and skill in the exercise of freedom.

If the individual is not to be submerged in the group or to pursue an anarchic or dictatorial course at the expense of the groups, then the manifold relationships of the individual and his fellows must be governed by a learned capacity to live creatively to the mutual advantage both of the group and the individual.

Skills in democratic living must and can be learned. As a result of the growth of trade-unionism in the automobile industry during the last twenty years, both the members of my own union and officials of the corporations with whom they deal have been educating themselves in these vital democratic skills.

This is a process which has no ending. It is not a preparation for democracy, it is democracy. And it should begin at the beginning, in the most formative years of childhood and youth.

This great need—to extend and deepen democracy by consciously elaborating democratic skills not only in the political field but in economic, social, and personal relations as well—offers an endless opportunity and challenge to our schools; to parents, teachers, administrators, and the children themselves.

Walter P. Reuther, President,
International Union, United Automobile,
Aircraft and Agriculture
Implement Workers of America

INDUSTRY SPEAKS

The need for continuing improvements of teaching and practicing all principles of democracy is indeed a virtue that is imperative for the American citizen of tomorrow. We in the aircraft industry, have seen the picture developing for a number of years whereby the needs of industry itself must be placed before our educators with the thought of revising existing curriculum to turn out graduates more flexible and more readily adaptable to the existing needs of our American industry with a well-balanced emphasis on both theory and practicality.

Woodrow McKissick
Senior Personnel Engineer
Boeing Airplane Company
Seattle, Washington

THE UNITED NATIONS ORGANIZATION SPEAKS

I think the type of teaching you describe is essential to our future success as a democracy, and I am delighted you have undertaken to write a book on it.

> *Eleanor Roosevelt*
> *The United Nations*
> *New York, New York*

There is no surer way to advance our democracy, to ensure the growth of our democratic institutions, than through education which consciously seeks to teach democracy, to convey to pupils and students its true meaning, to make democracy graphic to them and to encourage them to live by its precepts. For democracy in a society can never be stronger than the understanding, beliefs and practice of it by the citizens of the society. Without this, there can be no dynamic quality to our democracy and it will surely wither away.

> *Ralph J. Bunche*
> *The United Nations*
> *New York, New York*

GOVERNMENT SPEAKS

I have the strongest feeling that student participation in the learning process is the quickest and most effective method of teaching. This may only be a restatement of the fundamental idea that you learn by seeing, and feeling, and doing, much more quickly than merely by hearing.

Some reasonably conceived participation of students in planning of school events is also a desirable democratic experience and one which leads toward preparation for good citizenship.

> *The Honorable George Edwards*
> *Justice of the Supreme Court*
> *Lansing, Michigan*

Governor Adlai Stevenson of Illinois:

In a very real sense the central issue of education is the central issue of today: how a civilization which has reached, at least in America, unprecedented heights of material well-being and unlocked awesome secrets of the physical world is also to master the ways for preserving its spiritual and moral and intellectual values—for preserving, if you please, those very things that are the essence of civilization.

In a narrower, more political sense, the issue of education is how democracy can be made an instrument by which a people work together to mobilize the strength of the community to fight ignorance as effectively as we have fought every other enemy which has threatened us.

Yet crucial as these issues are, I would nevertheless emphasize first that any discussion of education cannot be cast just in terms of national needs, or a national policy or a national program. For education can serve the ends of democratic society only as it meets those of the individual human being. The essential condition of the system of free choice between conflicting ideas and leaders, which we call democracy, is that it be made up of all different kinds of people—which means that what we demand most of education is the development of informed people who are at the same time unique, different, unpatterned individuals. I think this means, in turn, that any national educational policy must encourage difference, experimentation and flexibility in educational practice.

President Dwight D. Eisenhower:
The Preparation of the Youth of America

First—To be alert and informed citizens, in an age when ignorance or misinformation could bring political catastrophe—an age when the guarding of our nearest communities may ultimately depend upon our knowledge of the most distant lands and peoples.

Second—To be tolerant and sensitive citizens—so that our society may not suffer the moral sickness that is bigotry—and may clearly perceive the values and the virtues cherished in other societies.

Third—To be skilled and accomplished citizens—able to grasp the great levers, turn the giant wheels, of this new atomic age, as nature finally surrenders to men so many of its colossal secrets.

Fourth—To be wise and reflective citizens, thankful for the new leisure promising a new freedom from much toil—not merely to relax in pleasure but to cultivate the mind and to nourish the spirit. To be wholly educated, in the sense that man is a spiritual and intellectual and physical being. America needs citizens strong in their ideals and spiritual convictions, healthy in their bodies, and tirelessly inquiring in mind.

And finally—to be bold and courageous citizens, knowing that strength and sacrifice are the indispensable saving weapons of freedom—and knowing that the frontier in America, that rules so much of our history, has become in this age, the frontier that is America—leader of free nations, hope of free men.

President John F. Kennedy:

First, we need to strengthen our Nation by investing in our youth. The future of any country which is dependent upon the will and wisdom of its citizens is damaged, and irreparably damaged, whenever any of its children are not educated to the full extent of their talents, from grade school through graduate school.

From the State of the Union Address
January 14, 1963

President Lyndon B. Johnson:

I propose that we declare a national goal of *Full Educational Opportunity*.

Every child must be encouraged to get as much education as he has the ability to take.

We want this not only for his sake—but for the nation's sake.

Nothing matters more to the future of our country: not our military preparedness—for armed might—is worthless if we lack the brain power to build a world of peace; not our productive economy—for we cannot sustain growth without trained manpower; not our democratic system of government—for freedom is fragile if citizens are ignorant.

We must demand that our schools increase not only the quantity but the quality of Americans' education. For we recognize that nuclear age problems cannot be solved with horse-and-buggy learning. The three *R's* of our school system must be supported by the three *T's—teachers* who are superior, *techniques* of instruction that are modern, and *thinking* about education which places it first in all our plans and hopes.

Specifically, four major tasks confront us:

to bring better education to millions of disadvantaged youth who need it most;

to put the best educational equipment and ideas and innovations within reach of all students;

to advance the technology of teaching and the training of teachers;

to provide incentives for those who wish to learn at every stage along the road to learning.

Message to the Congress
January 12, 1965

Does the task seem monumental? Let us simplify it by reducing our thinking to basic attitudes necessary to teachers using teacher-pupil planning. Let us think through our task in these terms:

1. Have faith in ourselves.
2. Have faith in our students.
3. Do not expect miracles.
4. Look for minor improvements; do not expect every day to be a day of major successes.
5. Keep our goals clearly in mind.
6. Keep in mind also the goals of our students, as individuals and as a group.
7. Do not allow a situation to get out of hand from a disciplinary point of view—keep the good of the group in mind.

8. Avoid major group conflicts, but establish the atmosphere of talking over problems together.
9. Use natural group influences: leadership, talent, comedy, skills of any kind.
10. Have the courage to try out new processes that suggest themselves to us and our students. Capitalize on enthusiasm.
11. Remember that criticism from your colleagues is often a high form of praise.
12. Evaluate constantly in terms of immediate and long-term goals. Evaluation reveals progress and looks ahead to better activity.

Today's teachers cannot be content to operate only within the wall of the classroom. We hold the key to answer the need expressed by thoughtful Americans. We are the technicians of education. We must not shirk this responsibility. Each of us must contribute to educational progress by daily action in our classrooms in finding better ways of working with our pupils, and thus, through our combined strength, finding better ways of living together.